GRASSROOTS CLIPPINGS FROM OKLAHOMA GREEN COUNTRY

GRASSROOTS CLIPPINGS FROM OKLAHOMA GREEN COUNTRY

A Democrat's Birds-Eye View of History Happening

Eleanor Franklin Sholl

Rev. date: 06/24/2016

CONTENTS

Acknowledgments 13
Introduction 15
Teen Pregnancy, Social Tragedy 17
The Social Science of Sex 19
God Loves Palestinians Too 21
Capital Gains Tax 23
Persian Gulf War 25
Election Issues in '91 27
The Politics of Abortion 29
Anita Hill's Credibility 31
Sexual Harassment 33
Homeless Veterans 35
Political Candidates for the '90s 37
Your Vote Counts 39
Carol Mosley-Braun 41
The Art Form of Politics 43
Candidate Debates 45
American-Provided Armaments for Foreign Wars 47
Democratic Convention—1992 49
Sexual Politics in America 51
Republican Convention—1992 53
Politicians' Character Issues: The Bush Dynasty 55
Joycelyn Elders 57
Waco 59
Health Care for Illegal Immigrants 61
NAFTA 63
Republicans' Slash and Burn Tactics 64
Welfare for the Rich 66
Whitewater 68

Make Health Care Equal 69
Nostalgic Movie Musings 71
Harry and Louise 73
Governmental Taxing and Spending 75
Newt Gingrich 77
Welfare, A Shared Responsibility 79
1994 Elections 81
I Am a Liberal 83
Newt Gingrich's Book.. 85
The Battered Wife 87
Bill Clinton's State of the Union Address 89
The Saga of Kelly Flynn 91
Abortion—Who Is Accountable? 93
Promise Keepers 95
Colin Powell and the Litmus Test 97
Government Shutdown 99
Who Will Care For the Elderly? 101
Flat Tax for Fat Cats 103
Raising the National Debt Limit 105
Support the Arts 107
Kemp-Gephardt Debate 109
Ernest Hollings on the National Debt 111
Al Franken, Political Satirist 113
Political Party Priorities 115
Bob Dole and the Character Card 117
Who Wears the White Hats? 119
Newt Gingrich and GOPAC 121
J. C. Watts' Response to State of the Union Address 123
Princess Di 125
Sexual Inquisitors 127
Can We Ever Get Along? 129
Yugoslavia 131
Jerry Falwell Bore False Witness 133
Music and Art as Cognitive Stimuli 135
Attempted Destruction of a
    President and His Administration 137

Gardening (and a Salute to Farmers) 139
Monica Lewinsky 141
"He Has Done Far More Good Than Evil" 143
Games People Play 145
What's Sauce for the Goose Is Sauce for the Gander 147
Steamroll Ahead 149
The Impeachment Process 151
Impeachment—Yea or Nay? 153
Hypocrisy 155
I Am a Gardener 157
Let's Cut Taxes if It Kills Us 159
Religion and Politics Don't Necessarily Mix 161
GOP Is B.A.D. 163
Tale of Two Cities 165
God and the GOP 167
Pork or No Pork? That Is the Question 169
What Kind of Society Do We Want? 171
Subliminal Political Advertisements 173
What's a Fair Tax? 175
Meeting of the Female Minds on Larry King Live 177
Oil Shortage 179
The World's Power Mongers 181
Violence in Entertainment 183
A Kinder, Gentler Newt 185
Pat Robertson and the Voter Guides 187
Ariel Sharon and the Peace Process 189
Whom Do You Dislike the Least? 191
The Public Relations War 193
No One Won This Election 195
Count the Votes for History 197
The Cards Were Stacked 199
One Man, One Vote 201
Wish He Were a Democrat 203
Something's Gotta Give 205
Oklahoma Pride 207
Pay Down the Debt 209

Postmortems 211
The Ashcroft Test 213
The Vision Thing 215

These letters are lovingly dedicated to Dylan Michael Whitaker, my great-grandson, born at the cusp of the 21st century in wonderful America, in the northeast corner of Oklahoma known as Green Country.

May he someday grow up to be a Democrat.

Oklahoma's Green Country

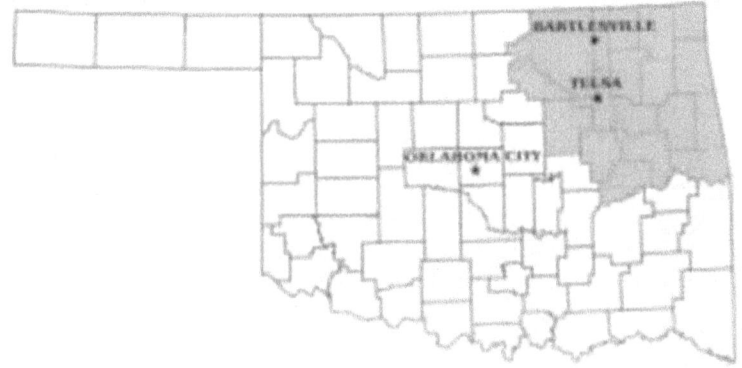

ACKNOWLEDGMENTS

My fascination with the political scene was inevitable because of the lifelong political activism of my late husband, Edward Sholl. He was first an idealist, and this morphed into activism.

I thank my daughter, Linda Brown, who is a partner in this enterprise. I have banked heavily upon her computer expertise. Long a connoisseur of language, Linda won the Washington County spelling bee two consecutive years when she was in junior high school. My granddaughter, Angela Sholl Kennedy, now in her first year of medical school, won the preliminary spelling bees when she was in junior high school, and went on to Washington D.C. to participate in the national spelling competition. Her father, Dr. David Sholl, was her coach, and thereafter became an accomplished and enthusiastic word aficionado.

Other writers in the family are my three sisters, two nieces (one is actually a first cousin once removed), and a brother-in-law who is a journalist. My greater family includes an awesome number of Scrabble and Boggle champions, and I know of four family members who complete a crossword puzzle every day.

Before his retirement, my husband invested in cable, for which I am grateful. I probably would never have thought of it, and would never have known what I was missing. Far from thinking my life would be so much better if only I could bring myself to ban television forever, I think of television as my university. Wonderful *CNN* and public affairs programs on all the channels are my meat and drink. They have brought the world to my door.

National Public Radio (*NPR*) and *British Broadcasting* (*BBC*), which run all night, are other food groups that nourish me. I find myself quoting something I heard on *NPR* with every other breath.

Feedback from readers of the *Bartlesville Examiner-Enterprise* (Bartlesville, Oklahoma) has been positive enough that I could decide in my own best interests to wield pen more and sword less.

I thank Joe Spann and Tri-County Technology Center for a course in small business which gave me invaluable resources with which to launch this enterprise. I am impressed that there are such resources devoted to the incubation of entrepreneurship and venture.

Joe Spann has nudged me toward *Epossibilities.com* and at last to the Internet. Eureka!

INTRODUCTION

These are letters to the editor that appeared in the *Bartlesville Examiner-Enterprise* over a period of time. I wanted to assemble them in book form for my own family archives, but I wanted to share them too, as a grassroots narrative of history as it happened.

I asked my daughter, Linda Brown, to be my editor and implementer. She is an avid reader, an English buff, and a computer software consultant. I have seen some of her clever product, and I wanted to cash in. Through her expertise, I wanted to tap into Internet publishing possibilities. It has turned out to be our best collaborative effort since she was born. It certainly beats circulating bulky manuscripts to disinterested editors for futile years, collecting pink slips.

Several years ago, my son, Dr. David Sholl, wrote observations of his several travels to India, and self-published his accounts. It was such a neat thing that I wanted to do it too.

Senator Joe Lieberman said recently of the two political parties: "We see things through different eyes." How true. These letters are commentary on recent events as seen through my eyes, those of a Democrat and political "junkie." They will be of interest to Democratic "true believers," independents and undecideds. They will not resonate with Republicans because they and I see things through different eyes.

I never discuss politics with people who have different views from me because it's not fun. My son, the doctor, is wonderful in every way, and he is my right arm, but we can never discuss politics. Once in an unguarded moment, I bespoke that Teddy Kennedy was one of our best senators. Startled, he rolled his eyes, and I quickly retreated from that thin ice, and so did he. I fear his children think of me as their eccentric grandmother.

No swing state, Oklahoma has for the last several years been firmly in the Republican camp, except for our state houses, which have always been safely Democratic. I have lived long enough to remember years on end when Oklahoma was uncontestedly Democratic. We've had two distinguished Democratic senators: Robert Kerr and David Boren. Rep. Mike Synar, a titan, was described by colleague Patricia Schroeder as a "tall tree in a forest." There have been two Democratic governors of recent years: David Boren and George Nigh.

I would be remiss if I did not mention Henry Bellmon, an outstanding two-term Republican governor of Oklahoma and a United States senator for many years. Those were years when politics were supposed to be civil, before the in-your-face, confrontational, Newt Gingrich-style of politics came into vogue. Bellmon was elected over and over because Democrats liked him too. He was much beloved by all, and Shirley Bellmon, his wife, was a class act.

Bartlesville, Oklahoma is the home of Phillips Petroleum Company, and is one of the Republican strongholds in the state. When I first moved here, it seemed to me that the ratio of Republicans to Democrats was about 50 to 1. Then I found there were actually more registered Democrats than Republicans in Washington County, and this is also true statewide. I love this spot of terra firma which is my hometown. I love the people here, Republican or Democrat. They are dear hearts and gentle people. As to the arts, religion, etc., etc., I have found kindred spirits. But I would have to say, for many of them . . . as to politics, we see through different eyes.

TEEN PREGNANCY, SOCIAL TRAGEDY

February 2, 1989

The State of the Union speech has been delivered and analyzed exhaustively, but there was one sentence which caught my ear, upon which no one has commented.

This came at the very last of the speech in the segment on welfare reform, at which time President Bush said in effect, "We've got to stop babies being born to unwed mothers."

If any political party can figure out how to do this, it has my vote on the basis of this one issue alone. In my opinion, the number one social tragedy of all time is children born into the world unwanted; children born to children, creating for both instant poverty; men fathering children without the ability or intention of supporting them.

I can think of one social agency which has as its objective exactly this: Family Planning. That's its name. That's its objective. They want to help couples avoid unwanted pregnancies. They want to help teens delay parenting.

I would suggest to this administration that one very positive thing they can do to stop babies being born to unwed mothers is to stop putting up roadblocks in front of this agency to prevent it from accomplishing its objectives. Stop making it illegal for doctors to counsel young women. Help overcome the conservative bias against sex education for teens. You can't have it both ways. You can't oppose every possible solution to the problem and then decry the problem.

It would be interesting to approach the welfare problem from this angle for a change. *Prevent unwanted pregnancies!* Once the children are here, there is not much we as a society can do except muddle along as best we can, which is what we are doing.

Somewhere along the line, there is the question of morality. If every generation of teens feels that sexual activity is their God-given right, regardless of the devastating consequences, what hope is there for society? To teens, early on, rather than say, "Don't have sex," I would say *don't make babies!* Plan to make babies when you can shoulder the responsibilities, and that is not the teen years. Every person has an obligation to society in terms of his or her own behavior. The President can't mandate, and Congress can't legislate that one.

THE SOCIAL SCIENCE OF SEX

February 10, 1989

I would like to make a social commentary from the perspective of one, who by this time, has had quite a panoramic view. My children were growing up during the sexual revolution, which meant that in my day, there prevailed what was known as the "double standard." By this was meant that the rite of passage for boys was sexual intercourse. With whom remained somewhat of a mystery, since at the same time, this was taboo for girls because they were the ones who became pregnant.

Society gave boys permission, because boys will be boys, and of course, part of growing up means sowing a few wild oats. It wasn't fair, of course, but that was the way it was.

Then came the Pill. Womankind was liberated! The playing field was level. Adults began having to take time out from other commitments to find themselves. It was a great time. Trouble is, it left us with quite a legacy of debris we're still trying to sift through. A Pandora's box was suddenly opened up. Teenage pregnancy is at an all-time high; children are having children. There are the accompanying problems of unwed teenage mothers, abortion and venereal disease.

Then there was another sexual revolution: AIDS. It turns

out that this is also equal opportunity. Maybe the ancient Judeo-Christian concept of sex as written in the Bible is the right one after all: "Keep thee only unto him (her) as long as you both shall live."

Wilt Chamberlain boasts of the 20,000 different sexual partners he has had. I wonder what has been the human cost to society of his behavior; how many children he has fathered whose care society then had to assume; what diseases he transmitted; and what lives he wrecked along the way.

I love Magic Johnson! He is a truly sympathetic figure. He was naïve. He was also profligate, promiscuous and dissolute. Is it really hard to figure out this is not the way we were meant to live?

I never expected to be in such complete agreement with Pat Buchanan on so many points. The mills of the gods grind exceedingly slow. The wages of sin is death.

GOD LOVES PALESTINIANS TOO

May 22, 1989

Plaudits to George Bush and James Baker for standing firm against pit bull Shamir and his Likud policy of settlements on the West Bank. The United States has vocally and emphatically opposed this action for twenty years, and Israel has proceeded, full speed ahead, in utter defiance.

As a nation, we believe in Israel's right to exist, and we contribute three billion dollars a year, including arms to the teeth, so that this can be possible. We are officially committed to the immigration of Russian Jews to Israel and have agonized with them for years as negotiations with Russia proceeded to this end. Suddenly the floodgates are open, and the Russian Jews are immigrating.

Settlements of the West Bank and Gaza are the chief stumbling blocks to peace in the Middle East. The arrogance of the Israelis on this point is unreal. They say, as the chosen people, God gave them this land 4,000 years ago, and therefore, they have the right to displace the Palestinians, who have been living there for 2,000 years. This having been accomplished with the blessings of world opinion, they will do everything to insure that the Palestinians have nothing—no homeland, no self-rule, no self-determination.

The mentality of modern-day Israelis is about like that of the Jews 4,000 years ago, who believed that they had a mandate from God to "go into this land and kill every man, woman and child."

As Christians, our affinity with the Jews arises from 2,000 years of common history. But we believe that with the dispensation of Jesus Christ, *we* are chosen. We are chosen, because we choose to be chosen, and no one is denied that choice. Christians, Muslims and Jews all worship the same God, but approach him in different ways.

I personally do not believe that God loves Israelis more than Palestinians. I rather think that God looks with favor upon the state of Israel, but I also believe in all fairness He wants the Palestinians to have a homeland also, with autonomy and self-rule.

As a nation, we should not be steamrolled by the big bullies in the Israeli leadership who stomp their feet and throw tantrums to get their way. Our commitment to them does not include agreeing to underwrite everything they want to do, as regards their hapless neighbors, the Palestinians. We are not committed regardless and no matter what!

Should needs elsewhere in the world always have precedence over needs at home? Why is it that anything we need here comes under the heading of "Tax and spend! Tax and spend!"? Foreign policy needs seem to have such urgency, we never ask "Do we have that kind of money? Can we afford it?"

With the Evil Empire now gone, what's the hurry to get all Jews out of there and into Israel? Why can't we put that on hold until there is some peace and stability in the region? Right now, the peace process with a fair shake to the Palestinians should come first. Perhaps Hanon Asrawi is a modern-day Moses, telling Yitzhak Shamir, "Let my people go."

CAPITAL GAINS TAX

September 30, 1989

I can't figure out what it is with the capital gains tax. If we lower it, that leaves millions and millions of dollars at the disposal of the upper 2% of the population, which they can then invest in factories and businesses which create *jobs*. It's supposed to trickle down into a rising tide that lifts all boats. Trouble is, how can we be sure that's what they'll do with all that money? Maybe that's what happened a time or two when capital gains taxes were lowered, but it certainly did not happen that way in the '80s.

In the '80s, all of that money did not go to expand and upgrade factories and launch new businesses. The people who profited from that tax arrangement started buying each other back and forth, and the rationale behind it all was that business would have to streamline and become really accountable to the shareholders. I've heard T. Boone Pickens very patiently explain over and over why he was performing a great service to all of us in trying to bring Phillips Petroleum to its knees.

In the '80s, all of that capital gains money did not trickle down. The upper 2% still have it. We have a trillion-dollar deficit which is getting larger and larger because the interest on it is the largest expenditure in our budget.

Now, George Bush, like Ronald Reagan, tells us unequivocally if the congress will just give him a capital gains cut, it will jumpstart the economy and bring us out of this recession—the recession caused by the last cut in the capital gains tax. I think our lawmakers are right in requiring that there be some correlation between income and outgo, but I don't think we can absolutely depend upon that upper 2% investing all of that money back in America. I'm afraid it's "déjà vu" all over again.

PERSIAN GULF WAR

February 27, 1991

Never pro-military, I am surprised to be so approving of our incredible military spokesmen. There is the unflappable Lieutenant-General Neal, who seems to have a real talent for public relations; the tough-as-nails General Kelly; and the absolute military genius, General Norman Schwartzkopf.

Most of the war stories we hear are serious, tragic, arguable and debatable. One was funny. It was about the Iraqi soldiers who surrendered to an Italian cameraman who had gone into Iraq looking for some good war pictures. Then a second group showed up, then a third. They all broke into a chant: "Schwartzkopf! Schwartzkopf!" Then there was quite a sizable group which marched into Saudi Arabia, inquiring of passing journalists where they might surrender.

While tactics were debated endlessly by journalists and specialists as to whether the Iraqi army could retreat with its hardware, or whether the Allies could go after the Republican Guards in southern Iraq, decisions were made and the war was waged. I think the world will be better off without Saddam Hussein. I can't believe negotiations with this madman would ever have solved a thing. However, I don't agree with President Bush that our noble fighting men were there in defense of our country, democracy and our way of life.

Most poignant was the story about our soldiers who were so

touched by the sad plight of the POWs that they scrounged around to find clothing (the POWs would get them officially, but later) and shared their finite food rations.

I wasn't gung ho for this war, and maybe I'm more isolationist than anything else. It seemed to me that George Bush was trying for a sequel to Grenada and Panama, and jumped into it without too much thought. Still, at this point, I'm addicted to the daily military briefings, and I'm impressed with the high caliber of our military men and women, including our wonderful, intelligent black soldiers. I saw one such interviewed after "killing" an enemy tank from an allied tank. He was asked, "Were you surprised?" "No," he answered, "That's my job."

Not too long ago, I saw a skit on *Saturday Night Live*, spoofing military briefings. The members of the press were asking stupid, repetitive questions, so inane as to be painful. The trouble is, you could substitute almost any briefing for the spoof, and it would be equally absurd.

Our top military men are smart, and are men of integrity and honor. I believe they are trying to win this war with a minimum of loss of life on both sides. Fielding the barrage of cynical verbiage they are subjected to every day should win them the Purple Heart for sainthood. The other day, several reporters were pressing the point that we should stop the war so Tariq Aziz could make it out of Iraq. How absurd! This sort of foolishness could cost American lives.

I'm still not gung ho for war, and hope we don't go out and find another tyrant to defang the day after this one. But . . . I want to salute the Tomahawk, the Patriot, all our wonderful array of precision weaponry, and our military personnel. All together now: "Schwartzkopf! Schwartzkopf!"

ELECTION ISSUES IN '91

April 24, 1991

From my position on the sidewalk observing this political parade, I am struck by a number of ironies.

President Bush is running on the premise that he is the candidate who would be a catalyst for change. If we don't like the way Washington is bungling things (and who does?), vote for George Bush, and he'll straighten everything out.

Mickey Edwards doesn't want to be identified with the sleaze of Congress. He went to Washington to clean things up, and by golly, that's what he's been doing!

David Boren wants a brokered Democratic Convention. He wants the Washington hierarchy to decide who would make the best president, who would be the most acceptable to that hierarchy, and then give that person the nomination. No matter that Lloyd Bentsen is the name most bandied about as "electable," and he just helped lose the election four years ago. None of these super-candidates had the guts to challenge George Bush when it would have helped. Bill Clinton has battered the bruising primaries and survived as victor to date. David Boren, this isn't your finest hour!

The problem is not only perks but pork. Robert Byrd is probably the all-time champion at this game, but everyone who goes to Washington seems to play the game, and if nothing else, bides his time until he can make his move. The appropriation committee skims off prime funds in every appropriation bill for their respective districts, regardless of what the original intent was, or whether the original problem is even addressed. See where the infrastructure projects really end up. The line item veto has been touted as the solution to this problem, but presidents practice this deviance too, and if the president is very partisan, forget it.

Sometimes I feel like Diogenes, who went around with a lantern looking for an honest man. Let's not make our elected representatives feel like they have to bring home the pork. Wouldn't it be wonderful if the "in" thing to do would be for them to say to each other, "I'll scratch my pork project if you'll scratch yours." If someone wants my vote, I want to know what he will do for the good of the whole country. That means less pork, less bureaucracy, and getting that deficit down.

As one of THE AMERICAN PEOPLE ™, I'm tired of being suckered. The whole savings and loan debacle was well-known to Washington insiders in the summer of 1988. But we were told nothing until after the election, and then it was fed to us bite by bite, so that it was several years before we knew its enormity. Now the bank crisis looms, but the game plan is to say nothing until after the election, and then the gory details emerge bit by bit, so as to get George Bush elected, and avoid anarchy.

Perhaps we can't afford to insure $100,000 deposits for everyone, and certainly not to reimburse losers $200,000 and more, as was done this time around. George Bush, it is too bad that all of Ronald Reagan's chickens came home to roost on your watch!

We need to change, all right. If that turns out to be Ross Perot, I'll show up to help celebrate. And yes, I think it helps for all of us to be mad as—heck!

THE POLITICS OF ABORTION

August 15, 1991

Who is pro-abortion? I'm certainly not. No one is. But as a woman, I would never have the chutzpah to issue ultimatums to another woman, even a daughter, a niece or a sister regarding what she should do about very private matters which should concern herself first and foremost.

We don't pass laws about men's bodies, and who would dare? Certainly not men! And who do you think will be passing laws relegating these unfortunate women to the status of criminals? Not, I assure you, a jury of their peers. It will be men, probably a bunch of old men.

It seems to me there is a little more behind this than the defense of the unborn. Retribution! She made her bed; now she can lie in it. If she didn't want a baby, she should have thought about that before the fact. Her behavior is the problem. Let's make it clear to women where their place really is.

Then, there is the slight inconsistency in passing laws saying to a woman, "If you produce a child while on welfare, we will reduce your benefits. If you have an abortion, we will pursue you as a common criminal."

The same people who are so determined that every little

fertilized egg produces a baby are the ones who could care less about child abuse, malnutrition or ghettos.

In how many instances do you think an unwanted pregnancy is caused by an aggressive female pursuing a hapless male? If men really wanted to do society a service, they would work on the aggression and chauvinism of their own sex. Little boys should be brought up to be a little less macho; less inclined to feel that any woman is fair game; less likely to use sex as power or punishment, or an act of violence.

If I, as a woman, would not invade another woman's privacy with laws and pronouncements, what do I think of a man who would do that? He is absolutely out of line!

My position is that this is not a matter for laws and the criminal justice system. If someone needs to be punished, leave that in the hands of God. "Vengeance is mine, I will repay." And from my knowledge of the Scriptures, I doubt seriously that God will be meting out punishment according to the formula some now envision.

ANITA HILL'S CREDIBILITY

October 15, 1991

The more I think about it, the more indignant I become over Orrin Hatch deciding Anita Hill was fantasizing as a way of explaining how she could possibly be so credible in her allegations that Clarence Thomas had sexually harassed her ten years ago.

This indicates to me a profound ignorance on his part about mental illness, an ignorance perhaps shared by many who have not observed this tragedy firsthand. I invite him, and any others who give credence to this theory, to visit a psychiatric ward, anywhere USA, and talk with patients there. You will find people with fantasies aplenty, fixations and obsessions, which to them are *reality*. In talking to them, you could not possibly confuse them with normal people who hold down jobs, buy groceries and balance the checkbook, not to mention teach in a law school and testify brilliantly for seven hours before a congressional committee.

If her statements were fantasy, they would be one manifestation of severe mental illness, and this manifestation would be one of many. Her general speech and demeanor would be affected; she would be extremely paranoid; she would likely personify the television, thinking its participants were talking to her, about her. She would have not one fantasy, but many. She would talk incessantly and too fast. She would say and do things completely inappropriate for the occasion. This is the tragic picture of mental illness. It is the picture of wasted lives, aborted careers and fractured families. It is a picture that, unless you have seen it firsthand, you would not believe.

Orrin Hatch, if you don't know about this shadowy world, maybe you should find out. I want everyone to find out. I'm indignant for Anita Hill, but I am indignant for the mentally ill too. The strong should bear the infirmities of the weak. You have to meet them, empathize with them, and try to do something to help. So far, for these afflicted unfortunates, they have an illness that has no cure. They are not to be confused with the perfectly rational people who say something that embarrasses you, and whom you elect to discredit in this way.

SEXUAL HARASSMENT

October 20, 1991

The whole sexual harassment issue brings to my mind a number of related issues. Hey, you guys out there, *the rules have changed!*

Camelot or not, I would never have voted for John F. Kennedy had I known thirty years ago that his main character description was "profligate." I'm not one of those Democrats who ever thought we just had to have a Kennedy in the White House, but who is smirking and winking at Teddy Kennedy's antics these days?

I used to have a Sunday school teacher who would preface a discussion with "When I say 'man,' I include 'woman,' because man embraces woman." As I grew up, in many contexts I would translate "man" as "mankind," and was never much bothered with sexism in our hymns and sermons. But I have come to believe it was there, and I am glad we have begun to address it.

Those men who, in their youth, considered that "scoring" or getting a girl pregnant was their rite of passage had better amend the rules for macho sons. From now on, a guy who fathers a child will support that child until it is 18 years of age. No more getting lost or ducking out.

From now on, if a girl says "no," better figure out she means "no," or else it's rape. No more trying to figure out ways in which it was really her fault. No more rationalizing, "She asked for it." The old ploys don't work anymore. And rape is a *felony*.

Women are now protected by law from sexual harassment. This law is particularly needed in the workplace. What passed with a wink and a nod, and "boys will be boys" ten years ago or twenty might land a guy in jail these days, or prove pretty embarrassing.

As to the Clarence Thomas brouhaha, it is interesting that members of the Senate are mad because the FBI report was leaked. Otherwise, Judge Thomas would have been confirmed and all of this could have been avoided. What a picture! Envision Patricia Schroeder leading a group of embattled congresswomen to the Senate chambers to defend the rights of women to a group of senators who don't dare come across as sexist. Anita Hill didn't offer any information until she was asked direct questions. If, ten years ago, Clarence Thomas had tried to pick a person to sexually harass verbally, the last person he should have chosen was one who would become a law professor, specializing in and teaching courses in minority and women's issues, including sexual harassment.

The lesson to be learned from all of this is an admonition straight from the Bible: "Beware, your sins will find you out!" Heed this especially if you expect to run for office or be confirmed to the Supreme Court!

HOMELESS VETERANS

November 12, 1991

In a recent national homeless symposium, I was made aware of something that disturbed me very much, and which I believe would make even the hardest of hearts bleed a little.

I was listening to *C-Span*, and I heard half-a-dozen very articulate homeless people give an account of how they became homeless. In these cases, all were veterans of one of our wars: World War II, Vietnam, and most disturbing of all, three were veterans of the Persian Gulf War.

The World War II veteran had held down a number of responsible jobs, had for a period of years earned $30,000 a year, and was paying on a five-bedroom house. Several of his jobs had disappeared in company layoffs or insolvency. He had lost everything, including his family, and was actually living in a homeless shelter. If it could happen to him, it could happen to anybody.

The Persian Gulf War veterans had left good jobs to go to the Persian Gulf, and sure enough, those jobs were not there for them when they were discharged. Nor were any others. One young woman had acquitted herself well in a responsible Navy assignment, and before that had held secretarial jobs; she was within eight hours of a degree, could not find a job and was in a shelter.

These people do not come under the heading of the mentally-ill homeless, the derelict homeless, the ne'er-do-wells, the addicts or the alcoholics. They are mainstream America. They are us. Of course, they would be faring much better if we weren't in a recession. But recession or not, something is terribly wrong if we can ask our young people to fight our wars abroad for whatever noble cause or political expedient, and then cut them adrift to sink or swim, and never really bother to find out which. I think we owe them more than that. If they have the ambition, the drive and/or the potential to return to the mainstream as productive, taxpaying citizens, we should red-carpet the road back for them.

Help for the homeless—that's a long, long process, because many of them are so hopeless. To digress, is this the best we can do for the mentally-ill homeless? But for now, just focus on the Persian Gulf veteran who is homeless. Most of them said, "We just need a little help."

It's a purely political matter. The people now elected have the power to do something. It's up to us to see that they do.

POLITICAL CANDIDATES FOR THE '90S

January 25, 1992

My television was tuned into Tulsa channel 6 last night, my interest in the Super Bowl being mainly when it would be over. I'm interested in the political issues and personally believe the Democrats have some very interesting and attractive candidates, including the Clintons. I didn't want to miss them.

I fell in love with Hillary Clinton. She is reputed to be a brilliant, successful lawyer, and may be another Elizabeth Dole, capable of being President in her own right.

Their interlocutor pursued his questioning relentlessly, as indeed he was supposed to. And I believe their answers were completely in line. Bill Clinton refused to say he had never had an extramarital affair, but it was none of our business. Their marriage is not an arrangement or an accommodation. They love each other and are committed and supportive. Hillary is no Tammy Wynette, just standing by her man. She believes in him. He's no John Tower or John Kennedy. I do believe that from now on, there will be reporters covering the side entrance of the White House.

It will be interesting to see if *the question* is a fair one for all the candidates. I wonder how George Bush would handle that one. When do the statutes of limitation run out? If you are a candidate for public office, you live in a glass house. But in this day and age (after the permissive '60s and '70s), where do we get all these people qualifying to cast stones? Furthermore, if you rattle the skeletons in my candidate's closet, it's only fair that I get to rattle the skeletons in yours. So go ahead . . . ask anybody. One thing for sure—it wouldn't pay you to ask Pat Buchanan. He may have beaten up a few guys, but you won't find *that skeleton* in his closet. I love the guy. He is *so* articulate. Too bad I agree with very few things he has to say.

YOUR VOTE COUNTS

March 16, 1992

The political battles are joined, my adrenaline is flowing, and it's hard for me to see how anybody can be indifferent to what's going on.

The healthiest state of affairs for our democracy would be one in which every citizen had an opinion which he felt an urgency to debate passionately with every friend and acquaintance. Wouldn't it be great if we had the 90% voter turnout in America that some of our more fledgling democracies have?

Anyone who is a television couch potato at all can be well-informed about issues and candidates, what with *C-Span* and public affairs programs proliferating on every channel. Watching them can become addictive, just like watching the Super Bowl.

How can anyone feel he has no voice in the affairs of our nation? How can anyone feel completely powerless? Every citizen of America can register and go to the polls and vote. If you don't like the incumbents, vote against them. If you don't like any of the candidates, vote *none of the above*. If you don't like the choices we have, join the groundswell for Lee Iacocca or Ross Perot, whomever you feel speaks for you. If you are completely disillusioned, all the more reason for voting.

I will admit there are plenty of reasons to be disillusioned. Take Rubbergate, as a case in point. These congressmen are so arrogant and so completely obsessed with their own perks and privileges that there is no time to be bothered with budgets, deficits and matters of national concern. Mickey Edwards is one of the 24 worst offenders. How long are we going to keep this guy around? Let's retire him at $100,000 a year.

Don Nickles tells us he has authored legislation to roll back the congressional pay raises. I'm with you on that one, Don. While we're rolling back, how about the retirement benefits for congressmen and ex-presidents? Isn't one million dollars a year in retirement benefits for Carl Albert a little much?

Why should the health plans for elected officials be so cushy at public expense, when millions of Americans have no access to our health system at all? I'm for our congressmen, state and national, playing by the same rules as the rest of us. Let's level that playing field. Sound like Jerry Brown?

Now for the partisan part. No Republican president is ever going to get elected without Democratic voters. I say to all Reagan and Bush Democrats: Come back to the Democratic party. All you disenchanted Republicans, welcome aboard also. (That's fair enough, isn't it?)

If you want Roe v. Wade to stand, vote Democratic. If you think the Supreme Court is packed with conservatives to the point of crisis, vote Democratic. If you are black and do not want to forfeit everything you've gained in the last 30 years, vote Democratic. If you benefit from or favor Social Security, unemployment insurance or workmen's compensation, vote Democratic. If you want to lump them together under the heading of "Tax and Spend, Tax and Spend," vote Republican. If you're willing to settle for what trickles down, vote Republican. If you think the sole function of government should be to create a military establishment, fight wars and police the world, vote Republican. If you think we'd be better off without any government whatsoever, vote Libertarian. If you don't care to have any voice at all as to what happens in our country and are willing to let your worst enemy make the decisions which most affect your life, don't vote.

CAROL MOSLEY-BRAUN

March 23, 1992

It's been quite awhile since I was moved to actually make a campaign contribution to a candidate. I did write a modest check several years ago; my candidate lost, left Congress with his war chest of several million, and now has lucrative employment in the fleshpots of the East. I have often thought I needed that money a lot more than he, but there's the gamble. If he had won, it would have been well worth it.

At the beginning of the New Hampshire primaries, I thought of sending something to Jerry Brown. He wasn't my choice, but I liked his populist appeal, and I liked what he was saying. I wanted him to keep on talking.

Now comes one who might well really spur me to action. Her name is Carol Mosley-Braun, a black woman who, in Chicago, has just won the Democratic primary for United States Senate. Her motivation for running was that the incumbent, Senator Alan Dixon, had been one of the handful of Democratic senators to vote for Clarence Thomas' confirmation to the Supreme Court.

If elected, Carol Braun would be the first black woman senator. That in itself would be history-making. But I like the fact that she was running in protest of the Thomas hearings and his confirmation. She portrayed the Senate as "an elitist club that is no longer representative of the people."

The reason for her victory was partly attributed to strong support from white women voters, thereby effectively challenging the male domination of the Senate and giving a boost to women candidates across the country. Yes indeed, an infusion of new women members would definitely serve to humanize, and improve the quality of product and accountability of that body.

Paul Tsongas said at his bittersweet finis, "Money is the mothers' milk of politics. Our mother wasn't there."

Carol Mosley-Braun, I would like to say that my check is in the mail, but I don't know where to send it. If only you had given us an 800 number!

THE ART FORM
OF POLITICS

March 30, 1992

The word "politician" should not be a dirty word. Politics is an art form, in performance of which some are found to be very talented and some not. Some hone their talents over a number of years and become very adept.

It is the art of coalescence and finding consensus. It is the art of compromise, because no matter how right you are, you cannot always have your own way. You have to be adaptable, because circumstances are constantly changing. You learn to be careful about what you say so as not to alienate a whole segment of your constituency. Ask Hillary!

Bill Clinton is a master politician. He's professional. One of his chief detractors is Paul Greenberg, award-winning and very right-wing columnist from Pine Bluff, Arkansas. One of his recent articles was titled "The Character Issue Just Won't Go Away." Of course, the principal reason it won't go away is Mr. Greenberg. He writes an average of one article a day on the subject of Bill Clinton, and the *Tulsa World* prints every one of them. We have him to thank for "Slick Willie."

I agree with Molly Ivins, 25-year political reporter of the *Fort Worth Star Telegram*, who recently spoke on the OSU campus. She trusts professional politicians more than businessmen, who may have very good ideas about how to save the country, but no political experience.

Lyndon Johnson was a master politician and knew how the system works, how Congress works, and started out fast-forward. Jimmy Carter, although he had a Democratic Congress, never did learn to work with the system. Having said this, I will also add that Jimmy Carter now has a persona and stature head and shoulders above any living ex-president.

Pat Buchanan bashes George Bush for not standing firm on the right-wing agenda. Hey there, Buchanan! Do you think a Democratic Congress is going to roll your conservative ideologies along? I assure you, if you ever were elected president, there would not be, swept in on your coattails, a congress of Vigurie clones. Thank goodness for checks and balances.

Molly Ivins is a very funny person with a broad Texas drawl, who, any day she decided she didn't want to write about politics, could make it handily as a stand-up comic. She's like Ann Richards, only more so.

Ms. Ivins thinks prying into a candidate's personal life is unproductive. The wrong question to ask George Bush is: Does he have a mistress? The right questions are: Does it make him a better president? Does it help him complete his sentences?

CANDIDATE DEBATES

July 10, 1992

I just caught my first candidate debate. My TV time doesn't always coincide with the program I want to see. I agree with Ron Brown; any one of these candidates would be good for the country. Any one of them would turn us 90 degrees.

I agree with Jerry Brown. The whole electoral process is flawed. Candidates become bought and paid for by the time they are elected. The graduated income tax is better, though. Why should Sam Walton pay the same percentage of tax as I?

I love Tom Harkin. He is feisty, witty and a scrapper. I would love to see him tangle with George Bush in a free-for-all.

Paul Tsongas is going to tell it like it is. No smoke and mirrors. How refreshing! Most of his ideas are solid as a rock. Somebody likened his face to that of a basset hound. If president, he might be something of another Abe Lincoln. He's for limited use of nuclear energy. In that, I agree with Jerry Brown, who would phase it out completely over a ten-year period, and Bob Kerry, who doesn't trust nuclear energy two feet. As Kerry points out, we haven't a clue as to how to dispose of nuclear waste, and until we do, we had better declare a moratorium on its creation. That might be for the next hundred years. Who was it, Kerry or Harkin, who thought that in 20 years, solar energy would be viable? I bet my money on that years ago. I hope it happens in my lifetime.

Newt Gingrich talked of the various wars of the last few years and said, "Democrats would never have done that." Is it really true that Republican presidents are more likely to go to war than Democratic presidents? If so, I'll vote for Bill Clinton because he is more likely to keep us out of war. He isn't so macho trigger-happy. You could count on him not to start a war to get our minds off of something he doesn't want us to focus on. Wars aren't always started for the noblest of causes. Sometimes the noble cause has to be thought of later. At least some of the "wrapping ourselves in the flag" is a little phony.

As for Mario Cuomo, he's the one the Bush forces would most like to face. They're all ready for him. These other guys scare them to death.

AMERICAN-PROVIDED ARMAMENTS FOR FOREIGN WARS

July 23, 1992

The graphic documentaries coming out of Somalia these days tell us of the enormous price of anarchy paid by millions of victims there, and the civilized world, which is called upon to bring order out of chaos.

At the root of the whole problem lies the proliferation of arms which has taken place over the last 25 years, not only in Somalia, but also in the whole continent of Africa.

When anyone has raised a voice to decry this state of affairs, we were assured that the manufacturing of munitions was a part of our gross national product, an export important to our balance of trade, and if we didn't manufacture and sell these products, other countries would, and we would be the losers.

Along with being policemen to the world, a role we seem to have whether we like it or not, we need to assume moral leadership also. A groundswell of public opinion needs to rise up and put an end to a number of outrages: the subsidy of tobacco products; allowing such products to be exported overseas; and above all, the manufacturing and exportation of munitions. I am sure we have paid for these armaments many times, even with our foreign aid, no less.

I doubt that it is much of an exaggeration to say that there are enough sophisticated weapons in Africa to arm every man, woman and child in that continent, and many of them were paid for with our tax dollars.

Why not outlaw the sale of weapons abroad and encourage our friends to do likewise? And after we have disarmed a million Somalian teenagers, why not try to do the same for the youth of our inner cities? If all of this mayhem is protected under the constitutional right to bear arms, maybe this is where we need a constitutional amendment.

DEMOCRATIC CONVENTION—1992

July 23, 1992

What a convention! What a party! What a ticket! As I watched the unfolding drama, I applauded, I laughed, I wept. I love to watch articulate Democrats verbalize what it means to be a Democrat! How's this for succinct? Bill Clinton's credo is to put people first. The credo of George Bush is to put *rich* people first. Ladies and gentlemen, I really believe that!

I had a favorite uncle who lived to be 96 years old, who, in the depths of the Great Depression, had voted for Norman Thomas. My uncle used to say, "The rich can pay for a doctor, the poor get service gratis, and the middle class just has to use Mentholatum!" In those days, most doctors served the poor of the community for free. My uncle would have loved the debates of the past few months, and this convention.

What an aggregate of titans the Democratic Party was able to assemble for this convention! I didn't hear them all, but I heard some real stars: Clinton, Gore, Cuomo, Bradley, Jackson, Wilder and Richards. Then there was Barbara McCluskey introducing the women candidates for the Senate, challenging among others Spectra, Grassley and Dole. I can see how Ross Perot would think the Democratic Party had its act together and was ready to move.

What fun they were all having! At one time, the camera zeroed in on a campaign button, "Democrats for Broccoli." Maybe that special interest group can attract some swing votes from Bush and Perot!

Then there was the brainstorm of the caravan. Here we see Clinton and Gore and their beautiful families shaking hands with America! What you see are family values personified! This is where I have been for a lifetime, and I am so proud to be a Democrat!

SEXUAL POLITICS IN AMERICA

August 2, 1992

I have known for quite some time that I was pro-choice (not pro-abortion, but pro-choice). I have cringed from the idea that Big Brother would have the nerve to usurp the regulation of the most intimate details of a woman's life and her body—and not just a woman's life and body, but *every* woman's life and body.

How far would any legislative body get trying to regulate the intimate details of a man's life and his reproductive functions?! Men wouldn't allow it for one split second, and you know it!

Well into reading the book by Marilyn French, *The War Against Women*, I'm beginning to put the whole problem into clearer perspective, and it is not a pretty picture. Males in a male-dominated society, from the simplest to the most sophisticated, assume that women alone produce children; therefore, these children are woman's responsibility to raise, to socialize, to feed. Often she is expected to accomplish this with no help, no reward and no consideration.

Fundamentalist Muslim religion gives women no rights or protection whatsoever, and even contemporary Jewish rabbis quote the ancient shibboleths, "Honorable women remain indoors."

Even in enlightened America, where women can vote, own property, be elected to Congress, and walk about freely in the streets, dressing pretty much as they wish, our Christian fundamentalists and right-wing politicos are busy trying to control them and keep them in their places. There is a great deal of indignation on the part of men that women would dare protest against sexual harassment, rape or abandonment, but in these areas, I believe women can and will be vindicated.

In the area of reproductive function, however, American males, even in the year of our Lord 1992, think it is their prerogative to dominate women . . . so we have a President, a party wing and a Supreme Court dedicated to this end.

After 4,000 years of patriarchy, i.e. male domination, some of these social mores are so deeply ingrained, particularly in the male psyche, they continue to resurface when least expected. What do women really want? I believe they want an end to patriarchy once and for all.

There is a war raging against women around the world, even in America. When the subject of abortion comes up, it's a woman's call.

REPUBLICAN CONVENTION—1992

August 30, 1992

If I were an alien from another planet watching my first political convention, I would get the distinct impression that this battle is being waged between right and wrong, white and black, good and evil.

The 1992 buzzwords, "family values," are about as phony as the 1988 flag huzzah. Did you ever attend a meeting called to order by these words, "Republicans will now recite the pledge of allegiance to the American flag"? Frankly, I have never known a Democrat who did not love his mother and apple pie.

I grew up in the Methodist Church in a Methodist preacher's family, and, thanks to my wonderful father, acquired by osmosis a sense of theology that has stood the test of time, never having to be revised or amended as so often happens. Early on, I was aware of the Jerry Falwells and the Pat Robertsons who are always with us, who claim an exclusive corner on truth and who are equally sure that no one outside their special persuasion even comes close.

What is amazing is that this particular brand of religious dogma could completely capture a political party so as to effectively become that party.

Newt Gingrich and Marilyn Quayle looked to me very much

like the Pharisee who prayed loudly from the housetop, "Thank God I am not as other men." Some humility! Christian theology includes the concept that if you think you are very, very good, you are, by that very thought, very bad indeed.

There is also the caveat to be pondered by fat cats, Republicans and Democrats alike, about camels going through the eye of a needle.

This convention was supposed to leave us with the belief that only Republicans have family values or are in favor of same. Somehow, I just don't believe that Saint Peter will ask to see a membership card in the Republican Party when we knock on those pearly gates. I have serious doubts that the separation of the sheep from the goats will be strictly along party lines.

This happened to a person I knew very well. Known as a political activist, he wore a button to work at Christmastime: "Happy Birthday, Jesus!"

One of the kidders at work said, "Hey, you don't think Jesus was a Democrat, do you?"

"Well, he certainly didn't come riding into Jerusalem on an elephant!"

No, Virginia, God is not a Republican!

POLITICIANS' CHARACTER ISSUES: THE BUSH DYNASTY

September 20, 1992

A nd now let us consider the character issue. First, there is
the other Genifer—Genifer Gerard. When the subject
came up in the 1988 campaign, George Bush, Jr. came to
Washington and held a press conference. He said about the "A"
word: "Nothing to it." That was the end of that. And of course,
this Genifer will never come forward. She has a job in
government.

Barbara Bush wants to leave the impression that she was a
homemaker who stayed at home and raised her kids. Actually,
she was the wife of a wealthy man, and she lived the life of a
socialite, a golfer and a member of the country club. Long before
she was First Lady, in answer to the criticism of the comfortable
Bush lifestyle, she replied, "We do live well. I don't apologize."
She's always had servants. I'll bet she never baked cookies in her
life.

Kevin Phillips is a political analyst, a Republican who has
served on platform committees. He didn't like what happened
in the '80s, and he is no fan of George Bush. He is the author of
The Politics of Rich and Poor, a book which rocked Washington

two or three years ago. It was the first of several books which showed that in the '80s, the rich got richer and the poor got poorer.

His commentary on *NPR* the other morning was that, as a family, the Bushes are the sleaziest of any presidential family in history. Both the sons and brothers are busy with questionable financial activities, which will, no doubt, end up costing the taxpayers money, just as in the Neil Bush fiasco with Silverado.

Not in that league, but nevertheless worth mentioning, is that Ross Perot made his billions with an electronics company which had lucrative contracts with the United States government to process Social Security and Medicare payments. These contracts were procured through contacts such as Jim Wright and other Texas lawmakers. They delivered to Mr. Perot the pork of an airport, paid for by the taxpayers, and he wants us to extend it at a cost of several million dollars. Nothing illegal here, but an example of patronage and pork. Not exactly the portrait of an outsider. Perot says he's not against government—just against waste!

JOYCELYN ELDERS

December 12, 1992

I would like to rise to the defense of Dr. Joycelyn Elders, whose recent firing from the post of Surgeon General was politically inevitable for a number of reasons, one of them not being that she did not speak the truth.

Dr. Elders is black and outspoken, which the particular white males who voted the Republicans into power in November would characterize as "uppity." She was rough-hewn, as you would expect a person to be who rose from her background of poverty, and she was physically unattractive, with a blunt manner of speaking which I am certain offended many on lower rungs of the ladder.

Her doctorate in pediatrics was attained after many years of clawing her way to the top. Hers was a Horatio Alger story if I ever heard one. The same qualities which caused Bill Clinton to appoint her Surgeon General of Arkansas, and later the United States, I still admire, but concede she could not have survived longer in Washington with the rising stars of Jesse Helms and Dick Armey.

During her two years as Surgeon General, a position largely symbolic and intended to be a bully pulpit, she spoke honestly about teen pregnancies, AIDS, violence and poverty. She was a pediatrician, and she saw firsthand every day what the rest of us only read about. She knew whereof she spoke.

"Truth as I see it and truth as you see it may be two different things, but certainly dealing with many of our poorer communities, I know their outlook on life is very different from someone who plans a trip to Europe every summer."

So what did she say? To fight the epidemic of teen pregnancies, she came out for sex education, and yes, condoms. What is your solution?

"We've tried ignorance, and that didn't work. Now let's try education."

She didn't volunteer to tackle the "M" word, but she was asked her views on masturbation, a loaded question if I ever heard one. In answering, she said she intended to convey her belief that masturbation is a natural part of human sexuality.

Wasn't Christine Tebby our first AIDS czar who was forced to resign because she said every human being is born into the world a sexual being?

You won't find an M.D., sociologist, psychologist or sexologist who wouldn't agree with both statements. To some, all professors in universities are left-wing nuts. I heard Bill Bennett say so at the recent Republican freshman orientation, sharing the podium with Rush Limbaugh.

Dave Barry, humorist, says, "There is no reason to be ashamed of our sexuality, unless you are Bob Packwood." I'll let Dave have the last word.

WACO

April 21, 1993

As I listened to the news conferences about the Waco tragedy, I was struck by the really dumb questions the members of the press were asking whomever. Questions can imply answers, but people on the offensive try and convict with the twist of semantics.

Imagine asking Janet Reno, Attorney General, if she would consider resigning in the wake of the Waco tragedy! Imagine asking if aides of President Clinton would consider resigning! Imagine the Republicans holding hearings to determine if this were somehow the fault of the Democrats! Imagine faulting firemen, who are trained to fight fires, not storm a fortress! Any compound which is stockpiled with ammunition forfeits the right to amenities of civilization such as fire trucks and firemen.

The only person whose fault it was is David Koresh. He was a ninth-grade dropout who not only considered himself the final authority in the interpretation of the Bible, but also presented himself as Jesus Christ. Undoubtedly a very charismatic person, he could outquote anyone from the Bible. Not everybody who says, "Lord, Lord" will enter the Kingdom of Heaven.

It was the fault of all groups who politically protect the right to stockpile lethal weapons. It could happen because our constitution protects religious freedom, and because of which we might find ourselves protecting cults, fundamentalists, crackpots, zealots and egomaniacs.

It was David Koresh who convinced his followers they would go to hell if they left the compound. It was he who ordered the fire and masterminded the mass suicide.

To quote from an editorial from the *Tulsa World*, "For self-appointed agents of God who do evil in his name, there must be a special place in the real inferno."

HEALTH CARE FOR ILLEGAL IMMIGRANTS

May 3, 1993

As we move closer to the unveiling of the National Health Proposals, some points seemed to have earned consensus well ahead of others.

There is the question as to who shall be eligible for the green card. Shall it be American citizens only, or shall we include the several million illegal immigrants in our midst, the number growing geometrically as we speak?

At first, the word was that this point had not been decided. It seems Hillary Clinton was opposed to their inclusion; Donna Shalala was in favor.

Next, the word is that it has been decided that illegal immigrants will not be eligible for the green card. Bravo!

California has a very generous package of health care benefits. It seems that hundreds of pregnant women come across the border to California to deliver their babies, so that the babies will be American citizens, and the hospital costs can be borne by the California Medical. Senator Henry Waxman of California has just introduced a bill into the United State Senate, which, if passed, would transfer this liability onto the federal government. Also, there are additional illegal immigrants flocking into California with other health problems: the need for surgery, dialysis, etc., expecting their health needs to be taken care of by Medical.

A good way to sabotage the whole health care system would be for people all over the world to come to America to get their transplants, AIDS care, or whatever. For America to become the world's great emergency room would come at a very high price.

It may be that once these people are in our midst, we have no other options than to give them basic care, but the green card— no. At least as far as bookkeeping is concerned, this expense should be on a separate ledger, so that if we go bankrupt with our health care delivery, we at least will know what is for our own citizens and what is because we can't solve the problems of our own borders.

NAFTA

September 20, 1993

Opponents of the free-trade pact with Mexico and Canada say that with NAFTA, jobs would move out of the country, and in whatever ways these countries would gain, we would lose.

Many economists, however, say that we would lose thriving export markets, cordial relations with our neighbors, and what we would gain is more poor Mexican immigrants. One study shows that if NAFTA is not ratified, the Mexican economy will go into a slump and 500,000 additional illegal immigrants will sneak north each year for the next decade. The enormous cost to us of this migration will be far more than the otherwise loss of jobs.

What NAFTA means to Mexico is social stability and sustained growth, which is exactly what we need Mexico to have, in our own self-interest.

Could it be that Ross Perot is actually wrong about something?

REPUBLICANS' SLASH AND BURN TACTICS

October 19, 1993

A s a passionate observer of the national scene (certainly not impassionate—jaundiced, perhaps—battered and bruised most certainly), and as one of the "American People" who are, as one purported to be, for this and against that, I would like to weigh in about a few things.

Republicans have killed Health Care Reform; Campaign Finance Reform (a bill which would have required stronger disclosure requirements on lobbyists); the Superfund Bill; and an attempt to rewrite the toxic waste cleanup law, all the while saying, "We didn't do it. The American people did it. They were not in favor of this legislation."

All of these measures had been years in the honing, and debated until the cows came home. They did not appear out of thin air.

Republican Mitch McConnell called campaign reform a "turkey" with provisions for financing that would have created an "entitlement for politicians."

Like the measure or not, the present system is a disgrace, and the people who want to keep the status quo do so because it is in their best interests. Democrat George Mitchell: "They are trying to be the beneficiaries of that disrepute (of congress)—tear down the institution so they can inherit the rubble."

Democrat John Bryant (re the gifts and disclosure legislation): "The Republicans have killed it. They have preserved their free meals and free tickets and free golf outings for two more years."

As for the Republican "contract with the American people," here is what they offered:

Lower taxes, especially for the wealthy, and on capital gains and inheritance. (Robert Novak is smiling.)

Reduced spending, the only specific being a "spending commission"! No specific budget cuts, no assurance that deficits don't matter. Specifics might include agricultural subsidies, Pell grants, potholes on highways, or sludge in harbors. American people, how specific do you want to be about these things? Somebody is going to have to decide where the cuts are to come from.

Columnist Jon Margolis created this speech for the hypothetically honest politician to deliver to the folks at home. "My fellow citizens, I pledge to you that I will not rest until there are fewer rangers in Yellowstone National Park, fewer firefighters in our national forests, and not a penny of federal aid for elementary and secondary schools. I will fight every Western water impoundment project. I will call for a reduction of air traffic controllers and the abolition of the Drug Enforcement Agency."

Republicans think "they" should "do something about entitlements." Do any of them have the courage to go home and say, "My fellow citizens, I pledge to reduce Social Security and restrict Medicare coverage"?

The present slash-and-burn, scorched-earth policy is the brainchild of Republican strategist Bill Kristol, most effectively implemented by Bob Dole, Phil Gramm and Newt Gingrich. The purpose of it is to afford Bill Clinton no victories, no success. Honesty? Integrity? Statesmanship? They have blood on their hands! Republicans, please don't offer these three to the "American People" as saviors of the Republic!

WELFARE FOR THE RICH

November 23, 1993

Thanks to computers, databases and talented researchers, we are constantly bombarded with all sorts of interesting data.

In this case, the number crunchers were Neil Howe and Phillip Longman, and this data appeared in a recent issue of *The Oklahoma Observer.*

Only 8% of federal entitlement outlays goes to those in poverty. In 1991, households with incomes over $100,000 received more cash and benefits from the U.S. Government than those families with incomes less than $10,000.

From 1980-91, benefits received by households with incomes less than $10,000 declined by 10%, while benefits received by those with incomes above $200,000 fully doubled. Those benefits included Social Security, Medicare and federal pensions.

In 1991, Medicare spent $19 billion subsidizing the richest third of all households, those with incomes of $50,000 or more. That same year, $9.2 billion went to military and civil service employees with incomes over $100,000.

Subsidies to farmers allow $50,000 on average to go to the 30,000 farmers with largest gross receipts, and two-thirds of total payments go to the richest 25 of the farms.

Should ex-presidents and retired congressmen really be entitled to a millions dollars a year in retirement benefits? We are all agreed that entitlements must be put on the table and examined for overhaul.

The conclusion of Howe and Longman was that what we have is a "welfare state for the affluent."

At least part of the rationale of entitlements was originally the elimination of poverty. The question is, what will it take to cut back or eliminate subsidies to the very rich among us?

WHITEWATER

March 1, 1994

Reading a recent editorial in the *Tulsa World* by Edwin M. Yoder, Jr., I at last began to make sense of the Whitewater hysteria.

The keepers of the national conscience were shocked, shocked, to learn that White House staff and other appointees had sought information concerning present charges and rumors, to see if they might implicate the president and/or damage him in some way. It would seem you might expect these appointees to take some interest in the well-being of the president, and indeed in less politically correct times, this would have been so.

But in these highly charged and partisan times, the times of Phil Gramm, Newt Gingrich and Bob Dole, let it be known that you must not meet. Bernard Nussbaum should have known that in these days "we do not permit meeters to meet."

These guys, if they smell blood in the water, they'll go for it. Washington has become so focused on the ethics thing, which by now is enmeshed in a well of fetishes and finespun rules and regulations, that whatever you do or whatever you might have done in junior high, they'll spin the rhetoric to come up with a plausible "gotcha"!

You're damned if you do and damned if you don't. Either way, they've gotcha! Politics is a dirty rotten game, but heaven help us, in a democracy, it's all we've got.

MAKE HEALTH CARE EQUAL

March 6, 1994

One of the reasons health care has been raised in the public consciousness as such a problem is that people are living longer than they used to. When Social Security laws were first enacted, life expectancy was around 50 years of age. People had diseases and died from them. The prognosis for most illnesses was not that good.

Now, medical science can do so much in so many areas that our expectations are far greater. People whose joints wore out 20 years ago spent the remainder of their lives in a wheelchair. Now, I can think of people by the dozens who are walking around with artificial hips and knees. Fifteen years ago, there was a procedure such as cataract removal, but implants that can actually restore your 20/20 vision were unheard of. Now, if you live long enough, you will have implants—count on it.

Most of us have someone in our families or among our acquaintances who would never be able to buy insurance. In the present climate, most assuredly, everyone will be able to buy insurance reasonably. Even short of universal coverage, there will be universal access, and that's a big improvement.

As a member of society, I am all for the best health coverage we can afford, even if it means more taxes. But for me, the absolute sine qua non is this: I absolutely want our lawmakers, members of Congress and government retirees to have the same health plan that all the rest of us have. We're the ones who will pay for it. Why should our elected representatives vote that we will pay for inordinately better health plans for them than they are willing for us all to have? I say, however this thing plays out, whatever the plan covers, or wherever we draw the lines, let's make it apply to all alike. That way, these makers of the law will scurry around and figure out something decent and acceptable, because they'll have to live with it too.

NOSTALGIC MOVIE MUSINGS

March 31, 1994

While watching Oscar winners Katharine Hepburn and Anthony Quinn in the television movie, *This Can't Be Love*, I was struck by the number of memorable Hepburn lines I can still quote, or almost quote, over a span of 50 years. Right now, there is not one single memorable line I can quote from any other actor of either gender, living or dead.

From 50 years ago, there was that Barrie play, *Quality Street*, or *What Every Woman Knows*. Franchot Tone was co-star, and it was a box-office flop, but it held the top spot on my charts for many years. Imagine Hepburn saying, "If there were just enough geese to go around, no sensible woman would ever get a husband!"

From *The Lion in Winter*, there is this scene, after family violence and mayhem unspeakable, in which Hepburn adjusts her skirts, smoothes her hair and muses philosophically, "I'm sure every normal family has its altercations now and then." This quote has not been researched for word-for-word accuracy, but hey—this is nostalgia!

From *On Golden Pond*, Hepburn is coping with the deteriorating mental condition of her beloved husband, a retired university professor, played by Henry Fonda. He is so rejuvenated by the serendipitous visit of a grandson that Hepburn opines, "If

I had known a 13-year-old boy could do him so much good, I would have gotten him one long ago."

I am sure there are dozens of other memorable lines. From the old Katharine Hepburn / Spencer Tracy films, there was the certainly memorable "Vive la différence!" But that line was inimitably delivered by Spencer Tracy.

And now comes *It Can't Be Love*. These two darling ancients meet after a separation spanning some 50 years and a fair amount of acrimony. At one point, Hepburn realizes she loves the guy, and imagine if you will, the quintessential Hepburn delivery of this line, "I feel as if I were 70 again!"

HARRY AND LOUISE

April 25, 1994

With Harry and Louise, their proverbial punch line "There must be a better way!" could be translated to "We're satisfied with things as they are. We're doing fine; don't change a thing; don't rock the boat."

Sure, "if it ain't broke, don't fix it" is OK for everyone for whom the system served up on order: dialysis, organ transplants, CAT scans, neonatal care, hospice, home health . . . you name it. But even for those people fortunate enough to have companies providing this fabulous coverage (no one could afford such coverage for himself), or to work for the government, so that shadowy monolith (meaning us) doles out such largesse . . . one way or another, it is accomplished at everyone's expense. We all pay for the system we have, which is certainly more than adequate for some of us, but therein lies the trouble. We all pay for a system which doesn't do much of anything for an awful lot of people.

Look at the people who oppose change and like the status quo. Invariably, they are the ones handsomely taken care of under the present system. Sure, they can't see there is a problem, because for them, there isn't.

Having said all of this, having laid bare my philosophical bent, I am sure you will not be surprised that I found the Bill / Hillary lampoon of Harry and Louise absolutely hilarious.

"Can you imagine? It says here on page 20344 that under the Clinton health plan, you might actually get sick!"

"Shocking!"

"And on page 31425, it says, eventually, we all are going to die."

Heads shaking in disbelief: "There must be a better way."

Then comes a cartoon with Harry and Louise now played by Bob and Elizabeth.

Elizabeth: "It says here on page 36344 that lowly taxpayers will have the same health plan as members of Congress."

Bob: "That's socialism!"

GOVERNMENTAL TAXING AND SPENDING

July 15, 1994

Tax and spend! Tax and spend! These words have been the rallying cry of a million political contests, and they have the power to strike such fear into my heart when uttered by the likes of Newt Gingrich that I cringe and cower into a corner.

Then the other day on *NPR*, I heard a political analyst speak to that point and so completely defang that phrase as to make it innocuous.

He said that, of course, governments will tax and spend. By definition, governments are entities given the power to tax and spend. If Democrats are elected to power, they will also tax and spend. If we have a Republican president, there will be taxing and spending. If Ross Perot were elected president, he would still have to tax and spend.

The questions are, then, whom will be taxed and what are the priorities for that spending? Herein is the framework for debate.

Take welfare reform. There is a man by the name of Krouse, I believe, whom I heard on *Crossfire* the other night, who has developed a plan. I like one point he made, among many. He said top priority should be given to programs which would take this great subclass of rudderless youth and lift them up into the middle class; programs like the WPA of bygone years; programs which would provide employment, training and skills. The GI Bill was such a program, and such a tremendous success, providing our nation with a whole workforce of skilled professionals.

Think what this would mean for our nation. What a middle class! What a tax base! This should be first priority, and then we could move on to accomplish other things.

Tax and spend! Tax and spend! But of course! That's what governments do. Now let's get on with the real debates.

NEWT GINGRICH

September 10, 1994

Who is Newt? Polls show that the name "Newt Gingrich" is far from a household word, and, in fact, most Americans could tell you little, if anything, about him. He is a former history professor, now a Republican congressman from Georgia, who barely held on to his House seat in 1992.

"Gadfly" is an adjective often assigned to him, as would be "highly partisan," "king of hyperbole," "loudmouth" or "junkyard dog." He is credited with having singlehandedly toppled Speaker Jim Wright by braying loud and long about trivia. Wright is now an articulate columnist in Fort Worth.

Speaking to lobbyists, Newt demonized Clinton as "an enemy of normal people," "normal" being anyone who agrees with his right-wing ideology, and feeds his political action money machine.

If Republicans gain control of the House, Newt, as Speaker, promises to impanel 20 committees (300 staffers) to investigate the Clinton administration, Hillary's cattle futures, and presumably Socks' cat food. If you like gridlock, you'll love the siege of terror under Speaker Newt.

On a political panel tonight on CNBC, Bill Kristol predicted sweeping Republican victories in the coming election, envisioning Bill Clinton working in a bipartisan way to enact the Republican agenda as articulated in its contract with the American people. "And then, hopefully, something will get done."

On this same panel, Democratic Senator John Breaux from Louisiana told of a woman running up to him at the airport saying, "Senator, please don't let the government take over my Medicare!" We certainly don't want the government running our lives!

In this new regime, Orrin Hatch would be chairman of the Judiciary Committee; Strom Thurmond, 81, would be chairman of the Armed Forces panel; Bob Packwood would replace Patrick Moynihan; and Al D'Amato would run the Senate's banking panel!

Republicans, this would not be your finest hour! Democrats, we could just win by losing!

I belong to a wonderful Sunday school class, which is certainly not, in Washington County, a bastion of flaming liberals. The study was Amos, and one of the questions posed was "Is God equally concerned with those who have a different culture and lifestyle? A religion different from yours? Recent enemies in war? Persons in your own country whose ways seem repulsive to you?"

Someone added, "Do you think God loves Newt Gingrich?"

Nobody had an answer to this philosophical question, but it broke us up. Class adjourned.

WELFARE, A SHARED RESPONSIBILITY

December 6, 1994

The debate continues to rage about what to do about the poor, whom we will always have with us, particularly the children and their unfortunate mothers. The fathers of these children are seemingly nowhere to be found, and, at present, Aid to Dependent Children depletes our national wealth to the extent of one percent of the yearly national budget.

For Christians, we might start with the hypothetical conversation between Everyman and Jesus at the Judgment.

"When saw I thee hungry and fed thee? When saw I thee naked and clothed thee?"

"Inasmuch as you did it unto the least of these my brethren, you did it unto me."

Believe it or not, this figures into the present political debate. The thesis is this: The government should get out of the welfare business and let the churches do it all. This has been their traditional role. This responsibility should be returned to them.

I was discussing this thesis with a friend, and he said, tongue-in-cheek, "Let's see . . . if every church took responsibility for two families . . . ."

Churches themselves do not have unlimited funds, and some churches struggle to keep their doors open. Add to this the fact that some churches are interested only in saving souls, and not actually helping people in more tangible ways, and you have a pretty staggering assignment for a few churches that are left that might be inclined to do something.

My father was a Methodist preacher in Sulphur, Oklahoma during the Depression. The churches were poor and the preachers were poor. There were no funds available anywhere for helping people in distress. Hordes of transients came through every day, unfortunate people who were down on their luck and trying desperately to get from here to there.

What was the plan of action of anyone interacting with these, the least of these my brethren? Why, to send them to the preachers, of course. We rarely sat down to a meal without a few guests. Believe me! As bad as it is, I like it better with welfare assistance, as we have now, so that all of us share responsibility for our unfortunate fellow men.

Another suggestion being bandied about is state-run orphanages. Been there! Done that! Although it would cost five times as much per child to care for them this way, as it does under ADC, it would have the advantage of seeing that no taxpayers' money got into the hands of: unscrupulous females who propagate irresponsibly; preteens; teenagers; whomever. Whatever the solution, this is our most gargantuan problem.

Back to my friend with tongue in cheek.

"Counties may have to operate poor farms once again."

At this season of Christmas, it would be most appropriate to open the pages of Dickens' *A Christmas Carol*, and say with Ebenezer Scrooge, "Are there no workhouses?"

1994 ELECTIONS

December 20, 1994

In the election of this past November 8, only 39% of eligible voters voted. According to exit polls, within this 39%, 95% of those who identified themselves as "blue-collar white males" voted to throw the bums out. Let's call them "*angry* blue-collar white males." They are credited with turning the election.

Do you really think they were voting for the "Contract with America," written by Newt Gingrich and Dick Armey, which has nothing for angry blue-collar white males, and which would immeasurably improve the lives of the most prosperous among us, and about which few Americans could tell you anything?

Let's face it, those most prosperous among us will never win an election themselves, because they are so few in number. So . . . they need lots of other very angry people to do it for them.

Of the 39% who voted, women voted overwhelmingly Democratic, and blacks did not vote at all. From this, you can conclude that blue-collar white males were angry, but the women who voted were not.

The blacks, politically represented by the Black Caucus and Jesse Jackson, who are considered the left part of the Democratic party because of their commitment to social change, had to be ignored by Bill Clinton, because that's what being a "New Democrat" means.

The "Old Democrats" (Liberals) are responsible for the Civil Rights Movement and whatever gains blacks have made the last half of the century.

One of the strong messages sent by this election was that blacks had better become politically active in a hurry or see all of their gains erased, which is what the "Contract with America" promises to do.

On all of the TV talk panels, I hear the black intelligentsia saying this very thing. I predict that blacks will become galvanized as never before, angry blue-collar white males will become even more angry, and their collective objectives will not be to eliminate the capital gains tax.

Arthur Schlesinger, Jr., historian, calls this document "A Contract *On* America." I wouldn't call the recent election results a mandate. I believe the jury is still out.

I AM A LIBERAL

December 20, 1994

I am a liberal. There . . . I've said it—up front—unabashedly. And since I am the one who called myself a liberal, you won't define me, thank you. I'll do that for myself.

Sexual orientation, or Woodstock and the mores revolution of the '60s, are not part of my bag and baggage. Very simply, I think that government can play a part in improving the lives of people. Government does have it's "raison d'être."

This is in contrast to the likes of Dick Armey, Republican senator from Texas, who is, to all intents and purposes, a Libertarian. He believes the only justifiable function of government is to provide for the national defense. I note that a goodly portion of the current body of lawmakers is of this persuasion. They couldn't get there fast enough—to the public trough, that is.

"Get the government out of people's lives," they say, except for women of childbearing age. These entities Big Brother must carefully monitor from puberty to menopause.

The GI Bill, after World War II, was a really great thing for America. Remember when Ronald Reagan was in the hospital from bullet wounds, he joked, "Hope these guys are Republicans."

Whether or not this was the case, the surgeon who performed the operation had become a doctor under the GI Bill.

However, this piece is not to be a rationale for liberalism. I just want to mention a few well-known people who are not afraid of the "L" word.

There is James Michener. He not only called himself a liberal, but a "knee-jerk" liberal at that. He was glad to pay taxes and considered it money well spent. He predicted that when he was dead, people would walk above his grave, feel the earth move and say, "There's old Jim. His knees are jerking again."

Paul Newman is very rich, and has been known to bankroll many liberal causes.

The parents of Kirk Douglas immigrated from Russia, and neither could read or write. Kirk taught his mother to write her own name and later give his production company that name. He's a flag-waving American and liberal to the core.

My list of liberals includes John Kenneth Galbraith, Arthur Schlesinger, Jr., Garrison Keillor, Barbara Streisand, Paula Poundstone and Roseanne. This is enough to show you I'm in good company. These people are all articulate about their liberalism, and I wish I had a quote from each.

However, I promise to continue adding to my list, and when I reach a thousand, I'll let you know.

NEWT GINGRICH'S BOOK

December 31, 1994

Gingrich Rejects Advance of $4.5 Million for Book. This headline is a part of an ongoing saga about a book, *To Renew America*, which Newt Gingrich, new Republican Speaker of the House, has yet to write.

It is based upon his course, required reading for all Republican office seekers, sponsored by GOPAC, his own personal pac. This pac enjoys tax-exempt status because it is claimed to be non-partisan and purely educational. It also enjoys anonymity of donors, which most pacs under present law do not.

Mr. Gingrich has served 22 distinguished years in Congress, and among his many accomplishments was the forced resignation of then-Speaker of the House Jim Wright, some 14 years ago.

Jim Wright had written a book from which he profited some $600,000, unconscionable and unseemly for an elected official. Several individuals had bought blocks of books, and to Mr. Gingrich, this appeared to be campaign contributions in disguise, circumventing new campaign reform laws.

Tony Coelho was also promised full congressional hearings on himself: his campaigns, business and personal life. Rather than submit himself to the Gingrich inquisition, Mr. Coelho promptly resigned.

HarperCollins, a New York-based publishing house which will publish Mr. Gingrich's book, is a part of the Rupert Murdoch empire, and Mr. Murdoch, an Australian, has an interest in major communications industry legislation to be taken up by Congress in the near future. I believe he has interest in acquiring Fox Studios, which present antitrust laws would not permit.

Enter Dave Bonior, incoming Democratic minority whip, who has problems even with the royalties. He also has problems with GOPAC's anonymous donors and its tax-exempt status.

"If I announced today that I was buying vanilla ice cream for every child in America, David Bonior would jump up and say, 'He wants them all to have heart attacks some day'," Gingrich said.

Seriously, do we want this to be part of the package? Elect someone to Congress, and in addition to their purported 16-hour days, they will toss off books which, because of their high profile, might be worth seven figures to someone who has business with the government?

Thank goodness for Dave Bonior!

THE BATTERED WIFE

January 17, 1995

As a feminist (one of those sensitive to the inequities women suffer anywhere in the world, or those banding together for the betterment of women), I reject Pat Robertson's definition (women who leave their husbands, kill their children and become lesbians). I would like to speak to the mindset prevalent in some parts of our society which makes it possible for men to beat their wives and lovers, and sometimes kill them.

I remember seeing an animated cartoon when I was a child, showing a man behind bars in a striped uniform, complete with ball and chain, who was pacing back and forth, and saying in some puzzlement, "She was MY Nellie!" MY Nellie! Who had a better right to do it?" He had killed his wife and couldn't understand why society would fault him for it.

Incidentally, my mother was a feminist long before the movement or the word. She raised four daughters, and we were not aware that women were second-class citizens until long after we were grown.

In the Muslim world, not by Koran but custom, men may kill the women in their lives: wives, sisters, mothers. This is accepted by society, and no law will bring them to justice.

Two thousand years ago in biblical times, patriarchy was the order of Jewish society and was much kinder to women than some of the pagan alternatives. Today, thank goodness, in our civilized society, laws protect women far beyond the beneficence of patriarchy.

It was therefore somewhat of a shock to hear Pat Robertson speaking in regard to the abuse and murder of Nicole Simpson: "She was *subject* to her husband." So, what's the big deal?

Anna Quindlen, in writing of O. J. Simpson in the *New York Times*, concludes, "He was not special, this public face. He was ordinary. He was typical." His wife-battering represents "a way of looking at the world and the women in it." Too many men share this outlook.

In a neighboring article, Mariah Burton Nelson observes that athletes are "especially disposed to attack their wives because sexism is a badge of honor in sports." She cited five cases of athletes who beat their wives.

Even in contemporary adolescent society, there is this super-macho pressure. Guys who have an egalitarian approach to the opposite sex are slapped with a crude label which I considered including, but was assured by the adolescent in my life that the newspaper would not print it.

In our society, many of our young men never become civilized. We must do a far better job in this respect. O. J. grew up a gang leader in a tough San Francisco neighborhood. He remained barbaric despite his wealth and success.

The abuse of women is now high-profile. I hope it remains so.

Men, in their network, could do a lot to change the climate. Just as "good friends don't let their friends drive drunk," maybe men should talk to their friends and say, "Hey, fella! You can't do that! You've gotta stop!"

Parents should fight "macho" in their sons. Macho means "Get what you want. Get what we tell you you want. Girls are ciphers. If you respect them, you are a wimp" (a much nicer term than the unprintable one). Those of you who wouldn't touch the word "feminist" with a ten-foot pole nevertheless know the kind of world and society you want for your daughters. And as you define that world and society, and work for it, let me assure you, you are a feminist!

BILL CLINTON'S STATE OF THE UNION ADDRESS

January 26, 1995

Bravo, Bill Clinton! You were magnificent(!) . . . a little long, but that was because you had so many lines that brought applause even as Republicans leapt to their feet. There were hisses too, and smirks from Dick Armey and Tom Delay, Republican majority leader and whip, respectively (not respectfully, most certainly!).

I was applauding, laughing and shouting, as I am sure were millions of supporters all across the country.

Christy Todd Whitman congratulated you upon sounding like a Republican, but you campaigned on these themes long before the "Contract with America." You were there first.

Republicans want an amendment to the Constitution requiring Congress to balance the budget, the implementation of which will take seven years. You are the first president to actually start the downward trend, make substantial progress, and prove it can be done. What's the point of a balanced budget amendment? I say, let's balance the budget and reduce the debt, and not leave it to our grandchildren.

The Contract wants to replay the '80s, which got us in the mess we are in today, anyway.

Republicans want less government and less bureaucracy. You

and Al Gore have actually downsized considerably and plan on doing more of the same.

Some kind of tax relief for middle-income citizens seems politically necessary whether or not we can afford it (in terms of debt reduction). To me, your proposal is appealing, in that it is targeted toward child-rearing and education. How pro-family can you get?

Some voters hold you hostage because you promised health reform and didn't deliver. Why didn't you deliver (?)—namely, Dick Armey, Bob Dole, the insurance industry, and Harry and Louise. You were the first president since Harry Truman to even *try* to do something. And because the ball is rolling, it will keep right on rolling. Ah, Harry Truman! He retired in Independence, Missouri, on a *modest* pension—the last of a breed.

Thanks for pointing out that members of Congress earned more in one month than people on minimum wage will earn in a year. This year, when Congress voted to apply U.S. labor laws to itself, it's good to note that legislation is in the works to modestly scale back exorbitant pensions Congress voted for itself in 1987, which would make virtually every retired lawmaker a millionaire, and more, in his lifetime.

Newt Gingrich describes himself as middle-class, so he needs the $4.5 mil. Too bad there is never enough for these guys.

The pundits, talking heads and spin doctors have called your administration a failure at every turn. You have accomplished more already than the two previous administrations put together. Paula Poundstone said it best. "They were counting his administration a failure before he even moved his socks from the suitcase to the dresser drawer."

THE SAGA OF KELLY FLYNN

May 23, 1995

The saga of Kelly Flynn, first woman B1 bomber pilot, currently being played out center stage, invites commentary in passing.

She committed adultery, not quite so innocently as she would have us believe, counter to one of the Ten Commandments, and hence a sin according to Judeo-Christian theology—but a felony?

It turns out that it is against Air Force regulations, in which court she was being charged. This too was somewhat of a puzzle to me, having the impression, perhaps through movies but also from personal observation, that this culture was pretty hedonistic, where pretty much anything goes.

After all, our army left hundreds of thousands of Asian-American orphans in Vietnam, in the wake of that war. I have personally known young army wives who became alcoholics in that culture. In that war, GI Joe was handed a condom, given a round of penicillin and a slap on the wrist.

What sifts to the surface is that these regulations went into effect about ten years ago, the rationale being that army families are so fragile, they need protection for the sake of morale and army readiness. Casual liaisons in the military community had wrought havoc through the years, and the preponderance of military personnel are married.

Whoever would have thought that the army would lead the way for family values? After the initial shock, you really have to hand it to them.

The questions remain, however—Is this evenhanded? Do men lose careers, as has Lieutenant Flynn?

The ancient Jewish laws as laid out in the Pentateuch admonished women to be virtuous and monogamous, because only in this way could progeny be traced through the patriarchal line. Men were not so admonished, and could have multiple wives, concubines and liaisons without being "an abomination to the Lord."

To this day, in Muslim cultures, the men in a woman's life— father, husband, brother or son—may kill her, if they so elect, with impunity, themselves acting as judge, jury and executioner. This is often done for perceived sexual offenses—even the flutter of an eyelash.

This is America, and what progress we have made! We're actually debating this on the basis of fairness and evenhandedness. As to Kelly Flynn, she may have lost an Air Force career, but she is now a celebrity, and she is not a loser.

ABORTION—WHO IS ACCOUNTABLE?

August 1, 1995

The two opposing views on abortion will never reach consensus, but there are some questions I have never had answered to my satisfaction.

I assume that the prime objective of pro-lifers is the reversal of Roe v. Wade, but what then? Do you think that all women who abort should be charged with murder? And what then? Do you think that all women suspected of being pregnant should be monitored from the moment of conception, and by whom? Do you think that doctors should report all pregnancies to a central data bank . . . perhaps to Pat Buchanan?

I have heard some hastily assure, "Not the women. It's the doctors who should be charged and held accountable."

At the recent Cairo conference, the Catholic Church conceded for the first time that overpopulation is a major concern in the world. They vetoed both contraception and abortion as solutions, however.

Dr. Joycelyn Elders incurred the wrath of that church by saying that a bunch of celibate men were deciding that issue for women. You could take the premise further, factoring in the Supreme Court and the Congress, and say those who consider it their prerogative to decide that issue for women are a bunch of old men.

The question really is . . . who should decide? Some of us believe "the women," of course!

I really believe that sexism and vestiges of patriarchy explain much of the pro-life rationale.

Even in my lifetime, not enough was known of reproduction and genetics, so the idea prevailed that a woman merely carried a man's child and did not herself contribute to the genetic makeup of the child.

The dictionary defines "patriarchy" as: (1) A system of social organization to which descent and succession are traced through the male line; and (2) The rule of a tribe or family by men.

In this system, women might be subject to men inferior in intellect and judgment. Once a woman is impregnated by a man, how dare she decide she will not be pregnant! She may have to drop out of school; fall into instant poverty, which may continue for the rest of her life; go on welfare for two years and be maligned by society as a deadbeat; or rear her child as a single person with very little help; but, come hell or high water, we must carry a child to term.

In the meantime, the man may go on to higher education, pursue a career, marry and have more children, and decide for himself for which of his progeny he will assume responsibility.

Some are suggesting that shame and the stigma of society should return as a deterrent to illegitimacy. Stigma is defined as a token of infamy, disgrace or reproach. Upon whom is this shame and stigma to be bestowed? The woman, of course. The man is nowhere to be found except as he sits in august bodies to make life-and-death decisions about women.

I was in a group discussion about this subject some time ago, and one gentleman, conservative through and through, made what seemed to me the definitive statement, "I am a man, and on the subject of abortion, I plan to *keep my mouth shut!*"

PROMISE KEEPERS

September 4, 1995

I recently read a very interesting story about "Promise Keepers," a fairly new movement sweeping the country—a movement of men—about 90% good, constructive, positive and wonderful.

It is made up exclusively of men. (I certainly have no objection to that.) One promise is absolute fidelity to wife and the support of children. (Yes! Yes! Certainly!) It promotes interracial harmony and the brotherhood of man. (In this respect, it has the potential of being really great.) It promotes deep and profound spiritual experience and growth. (What could be more basic or fundamental?)

What about the 10% of this movement that isn't so good? The movement enshrines patriarchy, a societal model responsible for many of the ills of our society today. The 20th century managed to shed many vestiges of patriarchy, but it still exsists in pockets of attitudes. Oddly enough, some Christian churches perpetuate these attitudes.

Four thousand years ago, patriarchy meant that the women who did not remain virgins until marriage and chaste after marriage could be stoned to death. Such rules did not apply to men, of course, because it was men who made the rules.

Promise Keepers urge men to be in full charge of the family, the household and particularly their women. Never mind if in some cases, she is actually better at handling the money, balancing the checkbook, and perhaps even bringing home the bacon.

In patriarchy, where there are women, there must be men keeping them in line, keeping them in their place, keeping them barefoot and pregnant, and being sure they do not have a voice or a vote. Regarding whatever gains women have made in their lives and status in the last 75 years, patriarchy has relinquished its stranglehold very reluctantly.

So far, Promise Keepers assure us they have no political agenda, but a march on Washington is in the works.

What I fear and foresee is a march into the arms of Pat Robertson, the Religious Right, and the Republican Party.

COLIN POWELL
AND THE LITMUS TEST

September 16, 1995

Colin Powell mania is sweeping the country, and everybody and his dog has an opinion about "Will he or won't he? Can he or can't he?" More and more, we are finding out what he thinks about the issues polarizing the country.

From interviews with Barbara Walters and others, we now know he is pro-choice, although he prefers that mothers put their unwanted children up for adoption. He is for affirmative action because he is not two-faced enough to benefit from such a program himself and deny its benefits to others. He is a fiscal conservative with a social conscience. He is pro-United Nations and pro-gun control. He thinks the government does have a responsibility to intervene with programs which might keep people from starving to death.

On at least three positions, his opinions run counter to the mantra required for anointment by the Religious Right. This poses a dilemma for them, because as far as we know, Colin Powell's life is exemplary in every way and embodies all of the values they keep talking about.

He hasn't written any sexually explicit novels or invested in pornographic films. He didn't divorce his first wife so he could marry someone younger, more photogenic and with a better résumé. One or more of these descriptions applies to all the candidates currently enjoying the blessings of the Religious Right, but they qualify for those blessings because they can chant the mantra, and Powell can't.

An arch-conservative like Bill Kristol thinks Republicans should embrace this person because of who and what he is, and what he could do to advance the cause of the Republican Party, rather than reject him because he can't pass the litmus test.

I, for one, hope Powell wins and the litmus test loses. If he wins the Republican nomination, admittedly a long shot, I will give Republicans credit for being smarter than I think they are, and I might be tempted to vote for him myself.

GOVERNMENT SHUTDOWN

January 9, 1996

On election day 1994, Republicans took great pride in the fact that 73 freshmen were (no kidding, I'm quoting them) "meaner than junkyard dogs."

While funding the government and eliminating the deficit within seven years are two entirely different things, not connected in any way, these freshmen, with Newt Gingrich as master strategist, decided to link them together in order to (again, I quote) "hold his (Clinton's) feet to the fire."

"We have the power of the pursestrings. Do it our way, or we'll shut down the government," became the mantra. For six months, we've been careening toward this train wreck.

I remember in the campaign prior to the election of 1980, Ronald Reagan promised to abolish Social Security. He found very quickly that it was a very popular program with a plurality of Americans, so he pretended what he really meant was that he wanted to shore it up in order to preserve it.

In exactly the same way, Medicare and Medicaid were programs headed for the auction block in the "Contract with America." Since it was not possible to eliminate them forthwith, Newt adopted the strategy of "allowing them to wither on the vine." Now, we have heard ad nauseum, "We're not cutting Medicare. We're preserving it."

According to Alex Adwan, senior editor of the *Tulsa World*, in actual dollars, the deficit peaked in 1992 and has been shrinking since, from $290.4 billion in 1992 to $163.8 billion in 1995. As a percentage of GNP, it has gone from 4.9 to 2.3.

Last week, *Larry King Live* featured three of the freshmen congressmen and five people who were furloughed or directly impacted by the shutdown. One contractor with the government through one of the national parks said he had amassed debts of $900,000 because of it. He asked the congressmen how they could justify the government shutdown with its devastating financial impact upon so many.

J. C. Watts, our black Republican congressman from Oklahoma, said, "Because we don't want this burden of debt on our grandchildren."

Again quoting Adwan, "There is something frightening about a vanity that says 'We, and only we, are right; no other viewpoint can be considered. We will keep our government out of operation until you let us have our way.' "

Funding the government and reducing the deficit are not Siamese twins joined at the hip. To connect them is a terrorist tactic and holds us all hostage.

WHO WILL CARE FOR THE ELDERLY?

January 12, 1996

Priscilla Parten, a Derry, NH woman, asked Lamar Alexander who would care for the elderly if the budget is cut according to the GOP pattern.

His answer: "We're going to have to accept more personal responsibility in our own families for reading to our children and caring for our parents, and that's going to be inconvenient and difficult . . . ."

The GOP's Medicaid Transformation Act of 1995 transforms Medicaid by eliminating its guarantee, and adult children earning more than the median income of $31,000 a year may be held responsible for the cost of keeping parents in nursing homes, with liens on homes, incomes and savings. Nursing home bills will be paid from the children's education fund or from the person's own retirement savings.

Medicaid now pays for 60% of our nursing home care because the $35,000 a year it costs each patient will eat up his assets until indigent.

Families do not resort to nursing home care for their parents except as a last resort. Most residents of nursing homes are too ill to be cared for at home, and these account for only one-fifth of disabled elderly.

Back to Priscilla Parten's question, "Who will care for the elderly?"; the answer "we" really means women—the daughters and daughters-in-law. It was Danny DeVito who threw momma from the train, not Rhea Perlman.

All of this character development for Personal Responsibility will accrue to the 66-year-old daughter of the 88-year-old mother, so that the politician's social issue becomes a woman's deteriorating life.

To quote Ellen Goodman, columnist, "As educational loans are cut, we are told to be responsible for our own children. As company pensions are fading, we are told to be responsible for our own retirement. At the same time, we are to be responsible for disabled parents and even grandparents."

It's very much a gender thing. "When politicians up there start talking about Personal Responsibility, they mean *our* responsibility (women's), not *theirs*."

"Men are from Mars, Women are from Venus" applies to politics too. Women are responsible for President Clinton's high approval ratings. They are more concerned about the social issues because they are the ones most likely to fall through the cracks and get the little end of the stick.

FLAT TAX FOR FAT CATS

January 23, 1996

What's good about the flat tax? Absolutely nothing unless you're a fat cat. Besides the 13% flat income tax on everybody, there would be a 13% sales tax on everything we buy. I certainly would not be better off. And think of those who have to spend 100% of their incomes on necessities! What a pile-on!

Patrick Moynihan, who knows more about the Social Security system than anyone, says that the flat tax, if implemented, would be the end of Social Security, Medicare and Medicaid.

Of course, the idea is supposed to be that funding for these programs would come from the vast revenues tapped by this tax. But remember who has to establish and fund these programs all over again: Congress! Don't bet on it!

What will be left after stabilizing the ruble—twelve billion here and twelve billion there for the five Russian countries which used to comprise the Soviet Union; bailing out the Savings and Loan; funding the ever-expanding congressional staffs; and funding the pension programs for government retirees: military, bureaucratic and congressional? This latter is said to be an unfunded liability of many billions of dollars, not even counted in our budget deficit.

The Social Security program is the one thing that is working. Let's don't fix it! Think of the many millions of recipients who are trying to live solely from their Social Security payments! What happens to them? Their sons and daughters will have to take over the burden of their care. Or else perhaps the welfare system, which itself, by now, is nonexistent in this brave new world.

We need change, all right. But let's start with congressional reform which Senator Boren is right now seriously trying to push. Every senator and congressman should not have a staff large enough to run a small business. We need to know what these guys are doing and make them accountable to us. And yes, I think it helps for all of us to be mad as—heck!

RAISING THE NATIONAL DEBT LIMIT

January 27, 1996

Rep. Dick Armey, R-Texas and majority leader of the House of Representatives, says legislation raising the national debt limit should be passed only if another pound of flesh can be exacted of the president. Since all agree on the goal of a balanced budget, this can only mean cutting deep and viscerally, like the jugular.

Apocalypse now! The Republicans in Congress actually have the power to make it happen. No one really knows what catastrophes might follow in the wake of such an event: market collapse, recession, world depression. The beginning of the chain reaction would most certainly be higher interest rates for the government and for us.

Oklahoma Republican Representatives Steve Largent and Tom Coburn say they believe that failure to balance the federal budget poses a bigger concern in the long run. Coburn has talked with financial experts and believes any hit the economy might take would be temporary. "I am going to have real trouble voting (to raise) the debt limit unless there is some agreement on a balanced budget."

Steve Largent believes that whatever he says and does is God working through him. Freshmen Republican lawmakers were told recently by former Education Secretary William Bennett, "You guys are doing the Lord's work."

To quote Robert Reno, columnist, "The strategy pursued by Armey and many of the more obsessed Republicans seems to amount to this: Better to burn down the government than not get your way. An inebriated motorist careening down the main street of town awards himself the right-of-way. This is what you might call the drunken driver / scorched-earth school of politics."

My reaction to all of the above is "Heaven help us!"

SUPPORT THE ARTS

February 9, 1996

The battle rages over whether or not tax money should fund so frivolous and peripheral adjuncts to our lives as the arts, and whether art and music are the first things to eliminate from school curricula when there is a budget crunch.

I would like to offer a few observations on the passing scene.

Plato, in his treatise on educating the young, held that music and gymnastics were the two very most important categories of knowledge and expertise, the basis upon which the maximum development of mind and body depend. Far from being frills and expendables, these were the veritable bedrock of human development.

Studies have shown that children taught music and art in the preschool years become better mathematicians and logicians in later years.

There have been some interesting experiments on background music as an aid to learning. Students who were concentrating very hard on learning a foreign language were given various types of background music to listen to while in study. It was found that the slow movements of Baroque music, such as Bach and Haydn, actually enhanced the learning process, while no other type of music did this: fast, rock and roll, big band or jazz.

A new movie, "Mr. Holland's Opus," starring Richard Dreyfuss, is the story of a man who taught music in public schools for 30 years. It is the story about the value of the arts, especially music, in the public schools and in the incubation of human beings.

At the end of the movie, fine arts are eliminated due to budget constraints in order to keep the basics.

Computers are fine. Everyone should be computer-literate. Reading, writing and arithmetic are absolutely necessary. But music and art actually help all of these get accomplished. Three cheers for the Bartlesville schools, one of the four or five schools in the state to have an orchestra and string program to have survived after all of these years. Awesome!

KEMP-GEPHARDT DEBATE

February 11, 1996

A most interesting segment of *Larry King Live* recently featured an informal debate between Republican Jack Kemp, the original supply sider, and Dick Gephardt, Democratic House minority leader.

What made the encounter truly unique was the civility with which these two made their points. It certainly appeared that the two are truly fond of each other, the best of friends, and the complete absence of vitriol was remarkable and a pleasure to behold.

Kemp authored the Kemp-Roth Bill, which in 1981 cut taxes and ballooned the national debt by a trillion, and counting interest on federal borrowing, increased the national debt by 3 trillion. This too at the time was touted as "tax simplification."

Kemp, unrepentant, is still making the same points verbatim as he did as a congressman in the early '80s, with the same points of reference: Lower taxes will free up money for capital formation; and, as the rich grow richer, companies will be formed, jobs will be created, the economy will boom, and prosperity will trickle down. A rising tide will lift all boats, and it will be "Morning in America."

The fact that it was tried in the early '80s (revenues shrank and savings fell, and the national debt ballooned into the stratosphere) doesn't seem to embarrass Kemp in the least. He still passionately believes his thesis.

When asked about the shrinking revenues which would result from a flat tax, Steve Forbes assures us that the resulting economic boom would mean increased revenue for the government coffers and prosperity for all. It seems like "déjà vu" all over again.

I wish I knew the name of the person who coined this phrase on *NPR* the other day when this subject was being discussed. She said, "I don't believe in the growth fairy." If you do, maybe you'd like to buy the Brooklyn Bridge!

ERNEST HOLLINGS ON THE NATIONAL DEBT

February 19, 1996

Senator Ernest P. Hollings, Democrat from South Carolina, has, along with Phil Gramm, a southern accent so thick as to be like a foreign language, hardly intelligible to the average person. Many years ago, he was a Democratic candidate for president, and always, if you could figure out what he was saying, he made a lot of sense.

"If anyone comes up with a seven-year balanced budget without a tax increase, I'll jump off the Capital Dome," he said the other day. "None of the plans they're talking about balances the budget or comes near it. Just the service on the debt is growing so fast, it's just not going to be possible without a tax increase."

Both Democratic and Republican administrations alike count the Social Security Trust Fund an asset that reduces the apparent shortfall of the budget. This is done despite the fact that it is illegal because of legislation written by Hollings and the late Senator John Heinz, and enacted into law six years ago.

"It's illegal and they know it. I complain and they shrug their shoulders and call it a unified budget.

The truth is, Social Security is paid for. Medicare is paid for. It's the general government, defense and the rest of it that's not paid for. And because it's not, interest on the debt is running a billion dollars a day. There's no amount of spending cuts and loophole closings that's going to produce a savings of a billion dollars a day."

The point Hollings wants to make is that the unified budget is not only dishonest bookkeeping, it's also illegal. So if the only way to make a dent in the national debt is to raise taxes, why do we keep talking tax cuts as if these will solve all of our national ills, including dandruff? What we need is a few more honest brokers like Hollings (and also former senators Tsongas and Rudman) who tell it like it is, and make us keep working the equation until we get it right.

We all want a happy ending to this story. Close your eyes and visualize this scenario. Old Glory is waving in the breeze, the violins are in crescendo, and Fritz Hollings is floating down from the Capital Dome!

AL FRANKEN, POLITICAL SATIRIST

April 14, 1996

Political analysts are unanimous in crediting the Republican sweep of 1994 in part to Rush Limbaugh. Democrats looked on in helpless dismay as he and his several million dittoheads framed the issues and hammered them home from their point of view, hardly challenged. There seemed to be no one articulate enough and charismatic enough to challenge Rush on his own turf.

All of that has changed. We now have a champion: articulate, charismatic and funny as all get-out. Al Franken, whose skills were honed on *Saturday Night Live*, has taken on Rush head-to-head, and things will never be the same again. Franken is called one of the most brilliant political satirists of our time, and he is deadly. His book, a bestseller on the *New York Times* list for many weeks, is *Rush Limbaugh is a Big Fat Idiot, and Other Observations*.

If you are, or ever have been, a Rush dittohead, you will not like this book. If you have lived through the arid years, hoping for a glimmer of hope from someone in outer space, this book will quench your thirst.

Particularly, Rush does not like the poor. They are like piglets feeding off the mother pig. Compassion for the poor is a phony game. Rush will have none of it.

"Given his feelings about the poor, you might find it surprising that Limbaugh has himself fed off the largesse of the government—in the form of unemployment insurance. Was Rush temporarily disabled? No. He filed at a time when he was able-bodied and spending his days sitting around the house eating junk food, too lazy to even mow his own lawn."

Rush Limbaugh called feminists "feminazis." Al Franken's a little sick of cranky Republicans who can't keep their own families together telling everybody else about family values. Newt Gingrich, Bob Dole, Phil Gramm, Pete Wilson and George Will have this in common: they've all been married one less time than Rush Limbaugh.

"Bob Dole says, 'I've been tested, and I have been tested, and I have been tested.' He might as well have been saying, 'I've been testy, and I have been testy, and I have been testy.'"

"If you get beyond the fact that Phil Gramm is ugly, mean, hypocritical . . . and drives his wife like a mule, he does have a certain folksy charm."

Al Franken was one of those featured on *Larry King Live* one night this week, and I wish for you that you will someday see him doing his "Al D'Amato." That's like saying "Shalom!"

POLITICAL PARTY PRIORITIES

August 27, 1996

I believe in citizen involvement in the political process, but I get so sick of the doubletalk, spin-doctoring, posturing and dissembling.

The doleful, acerbic Dole—I hope he is never president; Elizabeth—yes, Robert—no. From Phil Gramm, whose speech at the Republican Convention was arguably the most boring; who resembles a chipmunk (or is it a prairie dog?); and who is from Texas (but, come on, that is definitely not a Texas accent)—please deliver us. He also has a beautiful, brilliant wife. Her, maybe. These two consummate politicians, Bob Dole and Phil Gramm, who are as partisan as you can get, are already running for president in 1996. The prospect sends chills.

One way to contrast the philosophies of the two major political parties is this: The Democrats believe that the government should be involved in the problems of society, and help make the lives of people better. The governments of most civilized societies have social services. This is not unique to the good ole US of A. Try living in a country that has no social services at all, and see what you think then (like Somalia, for instance).

The Republicans think the government should never have any program for the purpose of helping people, and should not collect taxes for any purpose, but should nevertheless maintain a military, buy weaponry and keep their constituents employed, even with obsolete, government-subsidized industries.

A large number of our elected officials are millionaires, but on the Republican side of the aisle, unanimously the euphemism for any kind of social program that might conceivably help the little guy is "tax and spend." They demand that these same taxes support them lavishly with perks and privileges, and spend most of their energies garnering taxes for pork to take home so that they can keep getting elected.

I think Bill Clinton was elected because more people than not wanted a more activist government, wanted social services, and wanted to do something about the deficit.

Articulate Republicans are still preaching "trickle down"; they still think all domestic programs are obscene, and whatever problems they might concede we have could be cured by abolishing the capital gains tax.

As it is, Medicare and Medicaid are bankrupting the country because our tax money is paying for the enormous cost of artificial hearts, organ transplants, kidney dialysis, expensive surgery and the extension of life for three more months for people who are ready to die.

It is time to reprioritize our health objectives, and to pay the cost, because not doing it will cost a lot more.

BOB DOLE AND THE CHARACTER CARD

October 17, 1996

B ob Dole using the character card against Bill Clinton in the current contest for presidency poses some interesting theological questions.

My understanding of Christianity is that the ultimate no-no is to claim moral superiority for yourself. "I am good. You are evil. (I am saved. You are lost.)" Wasn't it the Pharisees who prayed loudly from the housetops, "Thank God I am not as other men" . . . ?

To say "I am good" is to commit an act of gross arrogance and pride. St. Paul observed, "All we like sheep have gone astray. We have turned everyone to his own way."

If Bob Dole is a good man and Bill Clinton is not, this would be for someone else to say, and not Bob Dole.

Gail Sheehy, author of *Passages* and other best-selling books, wrote recently in *Vanity Fair* that when Bob Dole divorced his first wife and abandoned his very young daughter, it was for an airline stewardess. He arranged for her to work as a secretary on the government payroll, although she could not type and had no secretarial skills.

The condo that Bob and Elizabeth enjoy in Florida, presented to them by Archer Daniels Midland, is an investment that has paid off handsomely through the years in terms of tax breaks and special favors.

Mother Jones magazine has labeled Bob Dole "The Marlboro Man," so effective has he been through the years at protecting the tobacco industry from accountability, liability, and damaging legislation. I am sure he was worth every penny.

Elizabeth Dole now has personal wealth of $4.5 million. This was not true in the years before she was president of the American Red Cross.

Bill Clinton is actually the more spiritual of the two men. He is a Southern Baptist. (How saved can you get?) Libby Dole is, like Hillary Clinton, a devoutly committed Christian. Bob Dole attends church in deference to her.

Bob Dole often quotes his mother saying to him, "Son, don't take away my Medicare and Social Security. It's all I have." You would think, with the financial resources of the Doles, they could spare a little for his aged parents. Come to think of it, how old are they at this point?

Next time some demagogue says "Vote for me—my character is so sterling," look for the feet of clay.

WHO WEARS
THE WHITE HATS?

October 29, 1996

James Carville recently told a roomful of campaign managers that the danger of character attacks is that "everybody is human."

Ellen Goodman wrote recently, "How do you compare 'human' flaws? In the presidential campaign, for example, how do you compare a husband who 'caused pain' in his marriage and repaired it, with another who walked out of his marriage with barely a word?"

Sure, it happened many years ago, but in today's vernacular, Bob Dole and Newt Gingrich would both be labeled "deadbeat dads."

Elizabeth Dole, in campaigning for her husband, carries with her a prop, a side-to-side rocker which she uses to make the point that Bill Clinton changes his mind from time to time. Ignored is the fact that Bob Dole, a lifelong deficit hawk, suddenly became a born-again supply sider in order to appeal to the fickle masses.

Ronald Reagan has been canonized because he had a political philosophy from which he never wavered, even when the ship was going down. To those who disagreed with his philosophy, this consistency seemed hardly a virtue.

I now quote from a recent *New Yorker* article about an obscure

British philosopher of this century. "If our idea of a political hero is to be that of an original thinker who had vision for his people—and then courageously stuck to his stated principles through thick and thin, the best example we will find in the 20th century is Adolph Hitler."

Bob Dole says, "Where's the outrage? Where's the outrage?" My observation is that there is plenty of outrage. Except for extreme partisans, the guys in white hats appear to be sprinkled here and there in both parties. Neither has a monopoly. Can you, in your wildest imagination, visualize a white hat on the likes of Dick Armey, Tom Delay, Newt Gingrich, John Boehner, Bob Dole, Phil Gramm or Jim Inhofe? There are heroes and villains on both sides of the aisle.

In a recent *NPR* presentation, David Frost distilled parts of many interviews with political figures. Richard Nixon said that from his years in the Senate, he knew few who retired richer than when they began their careers. This would be a very interesting criterion for judging the characters of political figures. I'll buy that!

NEWT GINGRICH
AND GOPAC

January 13, 1997

After several years of dissembling, Newt Gingrich has finally admitted to improprieties as Speaker of the House (involving GOPAC), but says it was unintentional.

Kevin Phillips, political commentator on *NPR*, said of this brilliant, savvy and seasoned politician: "An innocent he is not."

In the election of 1994, when GOPAC tutored all of the Republican hopefuls in how to win an election, they were given campaign manuals containing 100 very negative, pejorative words to use against all Democratic opponents. Used very effectively by Kay Bailey Hutchison and all, these words swept Republicans into office and dominance. Can you imagine Jim Inhofe coming off as one of the good guys? Can you imagine New Gingrich insisting that GOPAC was never political?

As much as any other, Newt Gingrich was responsible for the campaign theme that Republicans were the defenders of decency, morality and the American Way against those "Philistines at the Gates," the Democrats.

From his black-and-white world, when the young woman drowned her two young children in a lake, Newt came up with the theory that she did this because a Democrat was in the White

House! Put Republicans in charge and family values will pervade the land, and crimes will be nonexistent.

Republicans in Congress are circling the wagons around Newt. John Bochner, congressman from Ohio, said, "Newt's willingness to acknowledge an unintentional mistake is refreshing."

"About as refreshing as eggnog gone bad," says columnist Paul Greenberg.

When Newt Gingrich orchestrated the resignation of Speaker of the House Jim Wright, Newt said, "A Speaker of the House should be held to a higher ethical standard."

Let's see the Republicans take the moral high ground on this one.

J. C. WATTS' RESPONSE TO STATE OF THE UNION ADDRESS

February 11, 1997

In giving the Republican reply to President Clinton's State of the Union message, J. C. Watts, Oklahoma's native son, distinguished himself positively. He can deliver an impressive speech, he has charisma, and he has a winning smile, all of which he was critical of President Clinton for also having.

I confess I did not listen to him much past halfway, because then the speech became official Republican apologetics, which we all know by heart by now.

Watts is a rising star, but he has won his place in history by coining a phrase so colorful and original that subsequently, every journalist and talking head has repeated it to spice and season his own presentation.

A piece in the *Washington Post* profiling Watts as the only black Republican in Congress, quoted him as saying he found it hard, at the end of a long hard day in his district, to mask his contempt for "race-hustling poverty pimps" like Jesse Jackson, and Marion Barry, mayor of Washington D.C.

That phrase, right up there with "jackbooted thugs," will have a place in every quotable quote anthology from now on.

Again quoting from the Watts speech, it is the Republican mission "to limit the claims and demands of Washington," which call for "more power, more authority, more taxes."

Sack the welfare state, and substitute for that, prayer and "spiritual, traditional family values." Sounds like maybe he should be a preacher. Maybe he should just pray and let someone else pass laws.

Make no mistake—laws will be passed, and he will vote. The debate is what is equitable and fair to everyone, and not what is advantageous to Bob Novak.

This same political camp wants the government to withdraw from the problems of the poor and let the churches do it all. Anyone who makes no claims for compassion should be off the hook.

Just what is meant by "race-hustling poverty pimps"? Watts was referring mainly to his black brethren, but this would include anyone who thinks the government should be involved in solving the problems of the poor, the homeless, the hungry, the unfortunate. That's you and me, brother.

PRINCESS DI

September 15, 1997

My television viewing is limited to certain times and programs, but I confess, there are few points of view concerning Princess Di's death and amazing funeral that I have not been exposed to.

Having grown up in a country without royalty, and being painfully democratic by philosophy, I have always intensely disliked the whole concept of royalty, whereby certain people are supported by the populace, and take pride in never doing an honest day's work. Talk about corporate welfare!

As for Di, she was Prince Philip's idea of a suitable bride for Prince Charles. She was young and a virgin; a proper English girl. The marriage was arranged, consummated, and Diana forthwith produced an heir and a spare.

Only a few months old, Prince William was taken to Australia for their first trip abroad, and Prince Charles was taken aback that everybody wanted to see Diana and hear about her. No one was the least interested in Charles.

The same thing happened in Japan, where the phenomenon was called "Di fever."

At the time of his marriage, and to this day, Charles was and is in love with an old flame, Camilla Parker Bowles. At their first meeting (eons ago), she informed him that her grandmother had been the mistress of some King George or other, and offered to perpetuate the tradition. Prince Charles accepted.

Di was dumped; Prince Charles hated her intensely, and Queen Elizabeth decreed that Diana's name would never be uttered in her presence. This makes it all the more ironic that Prince Philip walked behind the coffin with the other men of the family, and the royal family was portrayed as grieving for Diana.

The one skill Diana honed during her sixteen years of marriage, and knew for certain she had, was the art of communication. She took that and ran with it; became the most photographed woman in the world; became a sincere disciple of Mother Teresa; and was buried with a rosary given to her by that holy woman. Her concern for human suffering was genuine, and she used her popularity to call this to the attention of the world. For heaven's sake, let's give her her due!

As for Camilla Parker Bowles, she had to stop going to the market because she was pelted with rolls. It is feared that if she goes again, next time it might be overripe vegetables.

Charles gave a big bash at his country estate on the eve of Camilla's 50th birthday, hoping thus to introduce her to the English public. Diana upstaged the event so that it hardly made the papers. Some pundit has said, "Camilla will not surface again in this millennium."

SEXUAL INQUISITORS

February 17, 1998

B ay Buchanan, conservative spokesperson on *Equal Time*, says her standards would call for the impeachment of a president who committed adultery.

I believe a society in which everybody claimed privilege of hedonistic behavior would be one of utter chaos. The level of civility in our present society is a result, as much as anything, of our Judeo-Christian concept—fidelity in marriage.

I do believe that for the Special Counsel and 20,000 journalists to become Alfred Kinseys and chronicle the sex history of any one of us is fascist.

I would hate to be put on the witness stand and be asked, "Where were you on the night of August 6, 1972?" I would hate for my answer to weight the scales toward life or death for another human being. My point is that lawyers can be zealous to the point of absurdity.

I can't think of any particular skeletons in my closet, but I don't want Ken Starr clones to be picking around, holding everything up for scrutiny, hypothesizing, conjecturing, theorizing.

Moral or otherwise, the sex life, experiences or history of any one of us should be personal and private, and not the business of someone with a political agenda or any other agenda.

Do we want all candidates for political office to pass the test of the sexual inquisitors before becoming senators and judges? Do we really want all of our elected officials to be Gary Bauer clones? Shall we delve into Bob Barr's sex life?

In the current climate, will there be a rush to confess? Maureen Dowd shudders to think of Rep. Dick Gephardt holding a press conference in which he professes that he has never done anything with anyone at any time.

Sexual indiscretions and adultery may offend us, but they are not impeachable offenses.

CAN WE EVER
GET ALONG?

March 12, 1998

There is an interesting Gaither song which may have profound implications. The rich and the poor will "treat each other like sister and brother, when we all get together in the Lord"—the same with the tall and the small, and several other categories.

This set me to wondering if the Israelis and Palestinians will treat each other like sister and brother even when we all get together with the Lord.

And what about the Serbs and the Muslims?

Some of my best friends are Republicans, but on the national level, there is more hatred and vitriol between the Democrats and Republicans than is healthy or comfortable.

Richard Nixon resigned for high crimes and misdemeanors while the Democrats controlled Congress. Now it is payback time, and with the Republicans controlling Congress, Bill Clinton must be punished for winning the election. Jesse Helms and colleagues, highly partisan, caused Ken Starr, highly partisan, to be appointed Special Prosecutor, with a mandate to "get the president."

I suppose every president from now on will be subject to the same treatment because it will ever be payback time.

I suggest that the reason Bill Clinton remains high in the polls is that the American people do not consider Ken Starr fair and evenhanded, and they are alarmed and appalled by the Special Prosecutor and his tactics.

Can you imagine the spin doctors on either side ever treating each other like sister and brother, even in the millennium?

It seems to me that, in their own self-interests, the Republicans (through Ken Starr) should keep their foul hands off Monica Lewinsky. Whatever she is or isn't, she doesn't deserve to be the pawn in these down-and-dirty political wars.

I still think America is the greatest country on earth, but does a democracy have to operate this way? I believe we should vote and be politically active, but surely we can stop short of hating the opposition. Surely we don't have to destroy our opponents—a little civility, please.

Maybe even now, short of the Rapture, we could all get together in the Lord and start treating each other like sister and brother. Amen.

YUGOSLAVIA

March 19, 1998

I'm partly pacifist. The part that isn't says that if we are attacked, of course we would have to fight to defend ourselves, and this also includes the Evil Empire throughout the Cold War.

I deplore what is happening in Yugoslavia. I applaud the heroes there who are trying to rescue the victims. I believe in every kind and quantity of humanitarian aid, but I do not believe in sending young Americans to die in Yugoslavia. Colin Powell believes if we are involved there, we could suffer as many as 10,000 American casualties.

The mountains of Yugoslavia are entirely different from the sands of the desert, and these people have hated each other for 2,000 years. After 10,000 American casualties, we still might not make a difference.

I do believe that the Serbs, particularly Milosevich, are the bad guys, and they are the Christians, which should give us all pause. They are systematically annihilating the Muslims, who, under the present rules of engagement, cannot even defend themselves.

On the other hand, the Muslim religion itself is certainly one of the **big** problems in the world today. Look at Iran. There are no moderate Muslims there. They hate Christians, and they hate Americans. We are the **Great Satan**. They export terrorism, they take hostages, they bomb the World Trade Center, and instruct their followers to kill whoever disagrees, as with Salman Rushdie, himself a Muslim—this all in the name of their religion!

Yugoslavia is a quagmire which breeds world wars, and it is a good place for Americans to *stay out of*. Should Americans be put under UN command? I certainly would not give an unequivocal "yes."

I'm glad I don't have to decide what we should *do*. What we should *not do* is commit American blood to the solving of their problem, even in the name of Christian charity.

JERRY FALWELL BORE
FALSE WITNESS

March 25, 1998

Jerry Falwell was guest pundit on *Equal Time*, and was asked
how he justified promoting the infamous tapes which
accused Bill Clinton of every crime in the book, including murder.
"I did not promote them," explained Jerry Falwell. "I just offered
them and said, 'Look into it'."

If he just pushed them and said, "Look into it," of course,
that's not bearing false witness.

In truth, we would like every adult male to be a wonderful
husband to a perfect wife. If every child born into the world
were a wanted child, taken care of and brought to maturity by
loving parents, most of the ills of society would not have come
to be.

Our sexual harassment laws do not make sex a crime. If we
outlaw sex, I submit we have really opened a can of worms. Such
laws or such interpretations just won't work. Every human being
has some kind of sexual predilection, life, history (even
earthworms, as has been pointed out).

As to public outrage against Bill Clinton, where do you think
those who are Democrats, ideologically and philosophically, are
going to go? Do you think you will find them rallying around
Bob Barr? Do you think we will all decide we are for vouchers,

the elimination of the IRS, and unbridled laissez faire after all? Do you think we will all go to the polls and vote Republican, because after all, they are "good" and we are "bad"? Don't count on it.

We will continue to vote for the guy who best expresses our ideals and aspirations for the human race.

MUSIC AND ART AS COGNITIVE STIMULI

August 2, 1998

For 25 years, I have watched with interest as evidence accumulated from numerous studies that, just as reading to young children is crucial to their mental development, the exposure to music and art at a very young age will actually make a difference in their cognitive faculties.

A day or two ago on *NPR*, I heard a person talking about a book he had written, entitled *The Hands*. I only regret that I cannot give you the name of the author, a doctor of some kind.

In the study of Lucy, our mother several million years ago, it was observed that her hand was not like our hands at all. People of that time had brains a third as large as the human brain today. As the human hand developed over the next millions of years, the brain grew tangentially.

The conclusion is that hands and brains are very interconnected.

The author became fascinated observing his young daughter as she studied piano, particularly the interaction of mind and body. He decided to study piano himself.

Many people are in occupations where they have to use their hands: hairdressers, construction workers, and people who sew, garden, or play musical instruments, etc. The author concludes that everyone should engage in some activity in which the dexterity of hands is crucial. Quintessentially, playing the piano fits this job description.

Now, all of you piano students, as you do your daily practice, you can take satisfaction that, in addition to whatever you are accomplishing, you are helping your mind to grow.

ATTEMPTED DESTRUCTION OF A PRESIDENT AND HIS ADMINISTRATION

August 7, 1998

I really believe that there are those answers which should be acceptable in a court of law: "yes," "no," and "none of your business."

Just as a man would never accept the legal assault on his body as many would consider appropriate for a woman, I think few people would welcome taking the stand and being grilled by a lawyer about any aspect of his sexual life or experience. This is true even of people who are morally as pure as the driven snow. Things you might even have difficulty talking about with a therapist, you should not have to experience the indignity of having probed very publicly.

Let us hope that the pendulum swings back the other way, so that people do not have to answer questions they should never have been asked.

As to right-wing conspiracy: maybe "conspiracy" isn't the right word. I don't believe that all of the people who are out to get the president have meetings, take minutes and hold conventions. But neither can you say these people are *not* out to get the president. In fact, they have been for years. Here are a few who come to mind: Richard Mellon Scaiffe; Jerry Falwell; Jesse Helms; Bob Barr; Pat and Bay Buchanan; Ken Starr; many lawyers; many talking heads; many members of the Religious Right; and many members of the Republican Party.

I sincerely hope that the American People, through the ballot, will hold the Republican Party responsible for the excesses and zealotry of Ken Starr as he has, through legal channels, relentlessly sought to discredit and destroy the president, Hillary, and this Democratic administration.

GARDENING (AND A SALUTE TO FARMERS)

August 27, 1998

As a gardener, what might pass as "avid" in the springtime months is definitely not "avid" in the dog days. I am out there every day watering something just to keep it alive, and for me, watering has never come under the heading of "fun." I marvel at how much time can be allocated to other things, once this is no longer necessary.

What makes the hot weather tolerable is realizing that this is the end of August, school has started, and soon will follow the football games, lap robes, and hot thermoses.

I have always thought that the fall flower garden was the prettiest, because what we have left are the "survivors." Some things will bloom now that have not deigned to do so before now.

Gardening always makes me appreciate the real pros. I had tomatoes for my favorite vegetable dish, okra gumbo. My two surviving okra plants produced a few okra here and there, but for serious gumbo, I really depended on those frozen packages of cut okra, blessedly available at the supermarket. I'm so impressed that someone has been savvy enough to grow all of these wonderful things. And the beautiful flowers I see in church every Sunday . . . . !

Through the years, I have often thought—how fortunate that I did not have to grow whatever I ate. When farmers have a bad-weather year, I can feel their pain. In good years and bad, fair weather and foul, I salute them.

MONICA LEWINSKY

September 9, 1998

This will not be an attempt to be an exhaustive review of all sides, because there are many who are very vocal and passionate in presenting views opposite to mine. Here are a few observations from my chair.

Monica Lewinsky came to Washington to "earn her presidential kneepads." The young lady who advises lawyers on the selection of juries characterized the situation as a setup for the president.

Orrin Hatch and other Republicans said, "Tell the truth, and we'll stand behind you." Almost immediately, it was a classic case of "bait and switch." If the president had appeared in haircloth and beat his breast, it would not have satisfied these partisans.

The whole mumbo-jumbo of perjury and the suborning of perjury, the legalese of which we are all so weary, was a result of entrapment. No object of investigation should ever be hauled before a grand jury to answer questions damaging to himself.

Rep. Dan Burton of Indiana called the president a "scumbag." Then it was revealed Danny had fathered a child, a son (now a teenager) by another woman while married to his present wife.

Henry Hyde says that impeachment proceedings must be bipartisan. The Republicans can't do it alone. They will need help from the Democrats. Yeah, sure! After forty million dollars and six years of highly partisan witchhunting, let's all proceed in sweetness and harmony.

What a jury to sit in judgment of the president! What paragons of virtue! Newt Gingrich! Bob Barr! Dan Burton!

Rep. John Conyers, a soft-spoken man with a southern drawl who is minority leader of the Judicial Committee, emerges as a shining star. Rep. Barney Frank, another member of that committee, has long been a star and is probably the most articulate man in Congress. Come to think of it, this is not going to be a steamroll.

If the president's defense needs more star power, I submit Alan Dershowitz or Paul Rothstein, both law professors; they are brilliant and feisty enough for anybody.

One casualty of the whole saga may be sex itself. Dr. Thomas Moore, psychotherapist, has written a book, *The Soul of Sex*, which presents the positive aspects of sex. Because we have come so far, let us hope we don't fall into the deep freeze of Victorianism from which we will not emerge for an eon.

"HE HAS DONE FAR MORE GOOD THAN EVIL"

September 14, 1998

Ken Starr has shoveled his report into vans and dumped it on Pennsylvania Avenue. I am furious on Monica Lewinsky's behalf that he demanded all of these lurid details from her in exchange for immunity from the Susan McDougal treatment.

Despite his cherubic smile captured on camera day after day, as he delivered his trash bags to the curb or opened his car door, he's got to be the meanest man in the world! He's the one who gathered the lurid details, included them in his report and delivered them, knowing that they would end up on the Internet and the front page of the *New York Times*, solely for the purpose of humiliating and denigrating the president.

Even the most benign and familial sex act, if described in detail with graphic reference to body parts involved, and then released to appear on the Internet and the front pages of every newspaper in the world, is going to sound pornographic.

My observation of the talk shows is that most Republicans in Congress are shocked, shocked, shocked! Those who can are rushing to claim sainthood, as did Trent Lott on the Senate floor, for having been faithful to their wives.

The truth of the matter is that this is not the only measure of character. On a recent *Both Sides* with Jesse Jackson, the two ministers of Foundry Methodist Church, where the Clintons attend church, were guests. One said of Bill Clinton, "He has done far more good than evil." Most of us would feel pretty good if this could accurately be the summation of our lives.

One member of the clergy said of the polls, "The American people love this man. (Not Republicans, of course.) The only other president in history of which this could be said was John Kennedy."

I have read many essays comparing Bill Clinton with the two sport heroes of the hour who have just broken a 37-year record. They are the men of real character. Can you say that brokering the peace in Ireland did not take character, or going to bat for universal health care, saving the Social Security system, or demanding fairness for all of us little guys in a million instances?

On *BBC NPR*, one commentator spoke of the Independent Counsel being out of control, and predicted that in the last chapter, Ken Starr would be disbarred for overreaching his mandate by a country mile.

GAMES PEOPLE PLAY

September 26, 1998

For years, his opponents have had a field day with Bill Clinton's reply to the question, "Have you ever smoked marijuana?" His reply was, "I tried it once, didn't inhale, and never tried it again." This reply unleashed a firestorm of guffaws that has reverberated around the world undiminished to this day. It was further proof that he was "slick."

America has a drug problem, many people still arguing that marijuana is benign, and that we should legalize it to accommodate those who prefer it as the drug of choice. Actually, we wouldn't have a drug problem if the same marijuana users who guffaw had tried it once and never tried it again. I think Clinton's track record is pretty good on this one.

What scorn has been heaped upon him because of his answers to questions about the definition of sexual relations! There have been debates about this since time began. On college campuses for generations, the question was, "What is a virgin?" There was general agreement that if there was not penetration, it didn't really count. Ask any octogenarian, and he will tell you this was true in his day.

When I have had occasion to counsel teens with raging hormones, I always said, "Don't make babies." Back in the olden days, there were the terms "making out" and "petting." I have heard counselors of youth suggest that a distinction should be made between intercourse and outercourse. After all, we do want our children and grandchildren to grow up to be fabulous lovers someday.

Bill Kristol has quipped that Republicans mainly favor the old-fashioned kind of adultery. This, I take to mean, involves a hotel room, a bed, and the missionary position. Now we see that outercourse is so much worse than intercourse; in fact, it's an impeachable offense.

A psychiatrist wrote a book many years ago called *The (Deadly) Games People Play*. Included among them were "Gotcha," "Ain't It Awful?", "Why Don't You?", and "Yes, But." I could add "Bait and Switch." They are deadly when played out on the national scene for political reasons.

WHAT'S SAUCE FOR THE GOOSE IS SAUCE FOR THE GANDER

October 6, 1998

Members of the Judicial Committee, with its Republican majority, voted to release the four-hour tape of the president's appearance before the grand jury and any other material they thought would be sufficiently embarrassing to the president, compliant with the public's right to know everything.

Henry Hyde, venerable and esteemed chairman of that committee, is, we are assured, the most fair and evenhanded of partisans, and the procedures he chairs will be bipartisan and completely non-political. So far, all of the Democrats have voted one way, and all of the Republicans another, and the Republicans have the majority.

The newest shoe to drop is that this same Henry Hyde (in 1965 as he was beginning his career in the Illinois state legislature) began a six-year affair with one Sherri Snodgrass while both were married with children. Henry quips that this was thirty years ago, i.e., a youthful indiscretion, and on this, the statutes of limitation have run out.

He was in fact 41, hardly youthful, and had four sons. Where adultery is concerned, is there really a statute of limitations? The now-Sherri Soskin of San Antonio said Hyde told her he was single. (He lied.) She declined to say when she found out otherwise, or if she then ended the affair. It becomes of utmost importance for us to know, for the duration of the affair, how many liaisons there were, who touched who, where, and what body parts were involved, if children were produced or any abortions performed. I feel the public has a right to know, and the information should be made available on the Internet.

A reminder to those who would cry foul: "What's sauce for the goose is sauce for the gander." Confucius say, "You cannot repeal ancient maxims in order to further political agendas."

The wronged husband, Fred Snodgrass, is a retired salesman now living in Florida. He is still furious that Henry Hyde broke up his marriage. Six years ago, Snodgrass told a tennis buddy, Norm Sommer, about the affair. Sommer went to *Salon* to expose what he called Hyde's hypocrisy. Some predict this will be the Year of the Skeleton. They will be falling out of closets all over the land.

Last night on *Rivera Live*, Tony Blankley and Joe DiGenova, Republican apologists, were livid, certain that the White House was behind this outing, and Rep. Tom Delay believes that there are further grounds for impeachment here. By all means, it should be investigated, for another $40 mil.

The editor of the online paper *Salon* was on the show by telephone, saying he had no ties with the White House and was not a Clinton supporter, and in fact, his magazine has called for the president's resignation.

Here is the question I wish to pose: Is the mote that is in my eye really so much bigger than the beam in yours? Or maybe, which beam is the biggest, yours or mine? For total fairness, no one who has committed adultery should be permitted to cast a stone, uh, vote.

STEAMROLL AHEAD

October 13, 1998

Many analysts have figured out that the reason Congress must steamroll forward with impeachment proceedings is pressure from the Religious Right. Present them with the president's head or else. Or else what? Or else they'll take their tricycles and go home? Or else they'll start a new party? Or else they'll vote into office even more bloodthirsty Republicans who *will* go for the jugular? Or all of the above?

I just heard Senator Mitch McConnell say, "These are the people most likely to send us checks. These are the people most likely to run out and vote."

Some have dubbed the Religious Right "the Jihad wing of the party." Do you know anyone in the annals of history more unctuous than Jerry Falwell? More self-righteous than Bill Bennett? More self-aggrandizing than Pat Robertson? Jerry Falwell is very proud of the fact that he has hated Bill Clinton for 18 years. Bill Bennett thinks the American People are corrupt because they do not rally in lockstep behind all of his moral pronouncements. Bill [Bennett] and Pat were dust in past presidential elections.

Some have identified another wing of the Republican Party as "the Hezballah wing." This would include the most partisan members of Congress, and Washington insiders, lawyers Joe DiGenova and his wife Victoria Toensing. (Take that, Herold

Remorez! Take that! And that! And that!) Of course, with Republicans in the White House, they had cushy jobs.

Some are stern parents to the President of the United States. "Son, go to the woodshed. I'll get my strap." Today, Eleanor Clift made reference to "Teleban Republicans."

What they all have in common is that they twice fought tooth and nail to keep Bill Clinton from being elected president, and now they see an opportunity to overturn the will of the people and force him from office mid-term.

Rep. Alcie Hastings, Florida, has filed for impeachment proceedings against Ken Starr for abuse of power. Rep. Hastings is a member of the Black Caucus, and is serious and articulate. I hope we hear more from him.

Blacks and Hispanics nationwide, and the Black Caucus are 90% behind the president because of what this administration has done for them. Three black congresswomen, members of the judiciary committee, are of the stature of Barbara Jordan. I can name two of them: Maxine Watters of California and Sheila Jackson Lee of Texas.

Jerry Falwell predicts that in the coming election, the Democrats will be buried in an avalanche. Now is the time for all good men to come to the aid of the party. Now is the time.

THE IMPEACHMENT PROCESS

November 17, 1998

Sean Wilentz of Princeton found himself in agreement with historian Arthur M. Schlesinger that the impeachment proceedings were contrary to the intentions of the Constitution's authors. He sent e-mails to other historians, and soon had heard from 300, and ultimately 400, all of whom deplored the decision to conduct an impeachment inquiry, saying it could leave the presidency "permanently disfigured and diminished."

"Although we do not condone President Clinton's private behavior or his subsequent attempts to deceive, the current charges against him depart from what the Constitution's framers saw as grounds for impeachment," they concurred.

The House action "creates a novel, all-purpose search for any offense by which to remove a president from office." The proceedings are "extremely ominous for the future of our political institutions," and the presidency is "at the mercy of the caprices of any Congress."

Another skeleton has fallen out of a closet, this time the closet of a Florida House member who was running on the "family values / more righteous than thou" platform. When confronted, he denied, over a two-day period, having fathered a child out of wedlock 18 years ago, but eventually did admit it.

The theological implications of this phenomenon never cease to amaze me. The two parties are political entities, not religious institutions. It's bad enough to hear a church say, "We're saved, and you're lost," but to hear candidates anoint themselves with sainthood because they are Republicans is absurdity unparalleled.

Larry Flynt, former porn king and editor of *Hustler* magazine, has offered up to one million dollars for the stories of young women who have been victims of congressional sexual predators. Big fish would be worth more than lowly freshmen. He "felt sorry for Bill Clinton, being accused by these hypocrites." At last report, Flynt had received hundreds of calls. I said "former porn king," because Flynt had to move over for Ken Starr, whom Arthur Schlesinger has dubbed the "top porn banana." Flynt considers the Starr Report much more pornographic than anything the inventive minds of *Hustler* writers have been able to come up with.

Playwright Arthur Miller sees many parallels between the contemporary sexual inquisition and the Salem witchhunts of yesteryear. Bill Bennett thinks the American People are corrupt because they do not agree with him, and Lauch Faircloth thinks we are dumb because Bill Clinton's polls are still high. Stay tuned.

IMPEACHMENT—
YEA OR NAY?

December 19, 1998

The Judiciary Committee of the House has just voted along strict party-lines to impeach the President of the United States, characterized by John Conyers as a "coup." Five of the Republicans who will vote to impeach the President in the full House were defeated in the November elections by Democrats, thus altering the balance of power between the two parties, making this a decision rendered by a lame-duck Congress.

When the Republicans won both houses in 1994, they characterized themselves as "meaner than junkyard dogs." That they have lived up to this characterization has been a matter of some pride for them. At the time, personalizing this label for me meant Newt Gingrich, Dick Armey and Tom Delay. Now I can add 21 more images to my junkyard.

This body came to this historic decision—the Republicans all voting for and the Democrats all voting against—in spite of the fact the American People had indicated in the November election, and also in the polls, that they are against removing this president from office.

In spite of the fact that Ken Starr has spent $50 million and five years, all impeachment charges stem from the Monica Lewinsky affair, which only surfaced in December of 1997. Under threat of 27 years in prison if she did not give the right answers to the grand jury, Monica Lewinsky testified that President Clinton had touched her breasts and genitals. That the President would not confirm this when the lawyers questioned him is the basis of all four counts of impeachment.

He believes he did not commit perjury when he said he did not have sexual relations with that woman, "sexual relations" being defined in every dictionary as "intercourse"; that definition was also in Monica Lewinsky's mind, as evidenced in the tapes.

Republicans insist he admit to perjury before they can absolve him of blame, the reality being that this admission would be exactly the ammunition Ken Starr has spent five years searching for. And most, when questioned, would follow up with the admission that, while this might in some way absolve the President, they would still favor resignation.

Henry Hyde, whose six-year youthful indiscretion in his 40s broke up a family, now thinks the President should resign to save the Democratic Party. In fact, his resignation would save the Republican Party from the wrath of the American People, who above all are judging the fairness of this procedure.

The thrice-married Bob Barr, a real pit bull in this junkyard, had called for the President's resignation long before we knew of Monica Lewinsky. Mary Bono thinks the President should be impeached and removed from office to send a message to her children. Lindsay Graham thinks, even if the Republicans lose both houses in the year 2000, impeachment of the President and his removal from office will have been worth it.

HYPOCRISY

December 20, 1998

We take the high road, you take the low road. Both sides are singing this song simultaneously, and at a high-decibel level.

"In impeaching William Jefferson Clinton, we have saved the Republic," says Henry Hyde (no kidding!).

There is the political right wing, and there is the religious right wing. They are not one and the same, but they are two different wings of the Republican Party, and they have shared one agenda for the past six years: Bring down Bill Clinton. Tools in their arsenal have included $50 million dollars in taxpayers' money, a special prosecutor appointed by the right wing, and a number of right-wing conspirators: Linda Tripp and Lucie Ann Goldberg, Richard Mellon Scaiffe, et al., and numerous political operators.

Six years produced a body of embarrassing, scurrilous data which was dumped on the Internet as a prelude to a debate in the House.

Larry Flynt, publisher of *Hustler* magazine, felt that those sitting in judgment of the President were not themselves without sin, and were therefore hypocrites. He offered up to a million dollars to anyone coming forward who had been involved in affairs with members of Congress. Four women have come forward saying they have had affairs with Bob Livingston, Speaker-Elect of the House.

Bob Livingston, thus cornered, confessed to infidelities in his 33-year marriage to his wife Bonnie, was given a standing ovation by his colleagues in the House and assurance of continued support in his quest for Speaker.

Maxine Watters said, "There is one word that comes to mind—'hypocrisy'."

Dr. Tom Coburn decided to pray about it. After 24 hours, support for Livingston seemed to be eroding, and to save his family the embarrassment of disclosures a la Clinton, he decided to withdraw as Speaker, and from Congress.

For that, Livingston was awarded Man of the Year by his colleagues. "He admitted it, like a man. He didn't lie under oath like the craven Clinton."

Before dropping the bombshell of his own capitulation, Livingston called on the President to resign. Clinton's support hasn't eroded. The Democrats bused en masse to the White House to tell the President not to resign.

As for Larry Flynt, he saw injustice being done and was appalled by the unfairness and hypocrisy of the whole sorry six-year spectacle. He could do something to dramatize this, and did so. Call him "lowlife" if you will; ethically, he rates above most Republican members of Congress in my books. He had nothing to lose, as his popularity ratings hovered at about—40. Maybe his role in this will raise the numbers by 10 points. Who knows? Maybe someday he will be Governor of Xanadu.

I AM A GARDENER

June 1, 1999

I am a gardener. I have gardened for many years, but usually have felt appalled, post-season, at the time that had been invested, oblivious, at the moment, to all other pressing matters. This year, I have given myself permission to garden and enjoy.

My mother and father were master gardeners of both vegetable and flower. I remember my father hoeing weeds in his domain of function, never dreaming he could hardly wait to switch gears in his busy day and get with it. My grandfather was a "Johnny Appleseed," planting everywhere, always with a packet of seeds in his pocket.

Every seed has its own DNA instructions for how to germinate and bloom; every flower has its time in the sun. My parents and grandfather were endlessly fascinated by the process, as am I.

Time stands still in the crazy, lazy days of summer. Sometimes I work diligently. Sometimes I just sit and absorb the sights and sounds. Without effort, I can reach a state of nirvana, and whole blocks of time can disappear into that black hole. I get the same pleasure in my yard as you get camping by a river or climbing a mountain.

Sometimes I birdwatch. Birds love the neighborhood. My

next-door neighbor has a birdbath and feeder, and I have tall trees and lots of earthworms.

One of the Debussy preludes portrays the sights and sounds of a summer night. That prelude is all about my yard at dusk.

LET'S CUT TAXES
IF IT KILLS US

August 22, 1999

The Republican Party came into the world to cut taxes. I have heard more than one of the party faithful say so on several occasions. If there were zero taxation, Republicans would still be assuring that amorphous entity, "The American People," that they would get the hand of big government out of its pockets.

Democratic Senator Daniel Patrick Moynihan, retiring in the year 2000, has a mind more politically analytical than any in politics today.

Twenty years ago, Jack Kemp ran on the premise that cutting taxes would increase government revenues. The fact that cutting taxes produced a trillion-dollar deficit didn't deter him in the least from making the same campaign speech four years ago.

I personally remember Ronald Reagan in the late '70s, promising, if elected, to dismember Social Security. Later, when elected, when he moved to do so, he found that the program was so popular, he had to back down. Social Security was a safety-net program passed in the '40s (without the help of one Republican vote) when Franklin Roosevelt was president.

It was Moynihan who, years ago, saw the Republican strategy shift from opposing specific programs to starving the government through tax cuts. Reagan spoke of "disciplining the child of government through cutting its allowance." It was Moynihan who showed that the deficits accrued when David Stockman was budget director under Ronald Reagan were deliberately engineered. One Republican senator, after recently voting for aid to the farmers, said to a reporter, "Stop me before I spend again!"

It was Moynihan who exposed the sham of amendments to the Constitution, "automatic spending cuts," and other formulas that would avoid tough choices. And it was Moynihan who noted that Social Security trust fund surpluses were being embezzled to mask the deficits of the government.

Thanks to Moynihan, I don't believe we could possibly make the same mistake again, of deciding to finance anything (Star Wars defense, upgrading the military, etc.) off the cuff, while at the same time disciplining the child of government by cutting its allowance.

RELIGION AND POLITICS DON'T NECESSARILY MIX

February 5, 2000

It's "déjà vu" all over again. Here we have another proof that it's dangerous to mix religion with politics. The tendency is to equate them. Some Republicans are so sure they're right, they claim the endorsement of God himself on their every pronouncement.

First, it was Newt Gingrich. (And we all know what happened to him.) He said the reason a mother murdered her children by drowning them in a lake was because the present administration is Democratic.

Now Gov. Frank Keating comes along and equates small government with the Kingdom of Heaven. (Try Somalia!) He told an ORU audience that the Democrats in the Legislature have "yet to get religion." He suggests that you cannot be both a Democrat and a Christian. This is from Newt's playbook. It has even been preached from some pulpits.

Later, when asked by a student what would be the best way to deal with the Oklahoma teachers' union, Keating said with a grin, "homicide"—this after Columbine and Fort Gibson! Keating says it was a joke, and it did indeed break up the ORU audience (no plaudits to them). OEA President Carolyn Crowder said, "If a student made that kind of remark, even in jest, he or she would be suspended for the rest of the school year. If a teacher made that remark, even in jest, he or she would probably be terminated."

Oklahoma's teachers are among the best in the nation. Ninety-six were recently singled out for national recognition. Mitsuye Conover, Bartlesville teacher, is one of four national finalists for Teacher of the Year.

Our teachers are so well-prepared that we furnish teachers to many other states. We're below average only in teacher pay.

Gov. Keating once left the state for greener pastures. He returned to Oklahoma only to run for governor. He has trashed the state at every turn. Another Republican national administration and he's outta here. On the other hand, let's not accommodate him.

GOP IS B.A.D.

August 10, 2000

Now we know. It was not Frank Keating, our litmus-test Republican governor . . . it was litmus-test former congressman Dick Cheney whom George W. tapped for vice presidential running mate. Keating and Cheney score perfectly in Republican conservative philosophies. Dick Cheney voted against everything during his years in Congress. He opposed the Equal Rights Amendment; a call to release Nelson Mandela (after serving 23 years in prison); sanctions against South Africa; Head Start; and any kind of gun control. Maureen Dowd characterizes his voting record as being to the right of the NRA and Newt Gingrich! Frank Keating hates teachers and public schools. He is at present trying to gut all of the wonderful programs which the Washington County Health Department is offering to young families and children.

My extended family is a political microcosm of America. We have views extending all across the political spectrum. About one of these programs, my sister said of her son, "Of course, you know, S—is opposed to any kind of intervention of the federal government in people's lives." That is so Republican—so Frank Keating!—so Dick Cheney!

A worker in another county spoke of having a 17-year-old boy enrolled in the Successful Families program. His girlfriend left their baby with him, and he wants to raise it. These same

Republicans who would fight tooth and nail against these programs want to make sure that no baby is ever aborted for any reason, medical or otherwise. They want to make sure they all get born, but babies, you're on your own when you get here! Problems such as teen pregnancy, abortion and child abuse are to be met with only punitive measures. Criminalize it. Make it a felony. Incarcerate. Build more prisons. Republicans are categorically opposed to anything that would conceivably help.

Litmus-test Republicans believe, along with Dick Cheney, that the only reason for the federal government is to provide an army for the defense of the nation.

The battle lines are drawn. If you believe the above, that abortion should be criminalized, that social programs are interference in people's lives, then the Republican Party is looking for you. If someone can figure out ways to ameliorate, I vote for that.

TALE OF TWO CITIES

August 27, 2000

For a political junkie like me, the tale of two cities, one in Philadelphia and the other in Los Angeles, was a pleasant diversion from the dog days of August, and a balance with the main focus, watering the flowers.

Philadelphia was the site of the Bush Convention, or rather, the Republican Convention. Bush convinced us all that he is a nice guy, and like Poppy, wants a kinder, gentler nation. If I had been an alien from outer space, I would have been sold! These were Republicans in sheep's clothing! Tom Harkin of Iowa said compassionate conservatism "is like trying to heat a cold house with warm thoughts." The really scary characters were hidden in the attic. Nowhere to be seen or heard were the hard-bitten impeachment managers or the self-styled junkyard dogs voted into office in 1992, courtesy of the Newt Gingrich playbook. Back then, I saw a documentary of campaign speeches, and they all said exactly the same thing . . . yes, even including Kay Bailey Hutchison, who should have known better.

Thirty years ago, I heard a Washington insider say that health issues were on the front burner. Claude Pepper of Florida thought up a great beef-up of senior health benefits, and it was voted into law. Trouble was, it was to be paid for by the seniors themselves, and they protested so volubly, it was quickly repealed.

I well remember when Hillary Rodham Clinton went before

a congressional committee to talk about her health plan proposals. Dick Armey was her nemesis, snarling and nipping at her heels, torpedoing every proposal as soon as it was floated. The junkyard dogs were the ones who defeated health care in 1993.

Understandably, not showcased in Philadelphia were Dick Armey, Tom Delay, Trent Lott, Mitch McConnell, Bob Barr, Orrin Hatch or Henry Hyde.

In Los Angeles, Jesse Jackson was vintage. He came up with two memorable lines, "Stay out of the Bushes!" and another which, unfortunately, I can't remember. (I have a sister who voted for Jesse Jackson for president, and a brother who once voted for Barry Goldwater!)

The mantra of Al Gore is "They're for the powerful; we're for the people." I truly believe that.

Joe Lieberman has this wonderful face, a quick wit, a wonderful family history, and a memorable campaign quip, "Let's win one for the Tipper!"

Among my favorite Ds [Democrats] are Molly Ivins, Maureen Dowd, Charlie Rangel, Barney Frank, Tom Harkin, Paul Wellstone, Margaret Carlson and Eleanor Holmes Norton.

I am a proud liberal, and do not consider the term pejorative.

GOD AND THE GOP

September 11, 2000

For some people, the parties are too much alike; hence, we have third-party challengers. For some, like me, the parties are readily distinguishable, as they have been forever. But I will concede the phenomenon of the two parties sometimes switching roles.

Used to be, the Republican Party was the one that claimed to be fiscally conservative, while they labeled the Democratic Party "Tax and Spend." Now it is the Republican Party that currently proposes to give away a surplus yet to materialize, making escalating debt again within the realm of possibility.

Once, the Republican Party was unabashedly Simon Legree-ish, opposed to Big Government for any purpose. Now that they're compassionate, they also want to save Social Security, educate our children, and shore up Medicare.

For years now, the Religious Right has claimed a corner on God for the Republican Party. First, it was the Moral Majority, brainchild of Jerry Falwell, who raised lots of money from people who were convinced they were contributing to Good versus Evil. Ronald Reagan and Don Nickles, among many, were swept into office because of the Moral Majority groundswell. Jerry Falwell got tired of political activism, and his mantle fell on Pat Robertson, who renamed the movement the "Christian Coalition." This organization has raised billions of dollars on the same premise, delivering voter guides to churches which were led to believe that elections were a contest with the devil.

Now, along comes Joe Lieberman, Democratic choice for vice president, and God is firmly in the corner of the Democrats. This year, the Republicans can't count on the "God vote," which at the least will be divided. Nobody is saying the Republicans can't have Him too, but He won't be that sure bet for fundraising. We have yet to see what will happen to the voter guides.

PORK OR NO PORK? THAT IS THE QUESTION . . .

September 13, 2000

Most recently, I heard Senator John McCain discussing the work Congress has yet to do this session. He said if the funding bills come out of committee loaded with pork, he will vote against them and urge constituents to vote out of office the elected officials who load with pork. It seems to me that this should be our battle cry. Of course, this would change the way Congress does business, and the first to go under this criteria would be Democratic elder statesman Robert Byrd of North Carolina, who has managed to pave the whole state of North Carolina in the years he has represented that state. "King of Pork," I believe he has been anointed.

More and more ironies emerge daily. One Republican mantra for years has been, "Too much government regulation!" During the Reagan years, and subsequently, much progress was made toward deregulating everything. Corporations were to voluntarily regulate themselves.

Now, we have airplanes grounded on the tarmac for hours, with freezing people inside, and persons getting killed because treads separate from tires. Government has certainly gotten out of our lives. It was President Reagan who actually cut the regulation which was in place for tires.

The other day, I heard one Republican congressman say, "In eight years, the Clinton-Gore administration has done nothing to protect the American public from faulty products and services." This is one of those issues, regulation versus deregulation, between which the pendulum swings back and forth. The pendulum has now reversed course. Even billionaires and traffic controllers need unpolluted air.

Candidate Bush has had much to say about morale in the military. There are 6,000 people in the military on food stamps. What a scandal! But there were 19,000 people in the military on food stamps during the Bush administration! As a matter of fact, this has everything to do with the number of children in military families. Stipends are added for children up to a numerical point. What do you think? Should we have that numerical point?

WHAT KIND OF SOCIETY
DO WE WANT?

September 14, 2000

I am an optimist. I think, as a nation, we are getting better. When George Bush, Sr. wanted our nation to be kinder and gentler, this was good. When George W. wants the conservatism of his party to be tempered with compassion, this is good.

If I judge the Republican Party harshly, it is because of adherents such as Robert Novak, journalist and talking head, who has become for me an archetype. He could just as well be a Libertarian, as far as his ideology goes, but he depends upon the Republican Party to keep lowering his taxes.

Ayn Rand, in her novels, suggested "utopia" as being when everyone acts in his own self-interest. To her, this will create the best society. Robert Novak is one of many who espouse this philosophy. Contrast this with the admonition possibly familiar to some: "The strong should bear the infirmities of the weak."

"Every fellow for himself and the devil take the hindmost." Do we want that kind of society? I think we pretty much decided that after the robber barons. It's the kind of society Russia has today. The oligarchs siphon off the treasure of the nation and foreign aid into Swiss bank accounts with no laws to keep it from happening, while the people become poorer and poorer.

We have 400 billionaires in this country, and thousands of millionaires who have become so because they, like we, live in the greatest country in the history of the world. We have a huge middle class which no other country in any age has ever had.

The upper 20 percent pay 80 percent of the taxes, which comprise 40 percent of their incomes. They would get most of the tax relief which George W. proposes. "Why shouldn't they?" I heard John Kasich say. "They pay most of the taxes." "They're the ones who create the jobs," says Mary Matalin. It's the same trickle-down theory that didn't work 20 years ago. Jack Kemp is still passionate in his defense of it. "Look at our prosperity now," he says. "That proves it did work."

Also, the big tax cut which has been proposed is for a projected surplus over the next ten years, which may or may not materialize. The budget is balanced, but we still have this huge debt from the last trickle-down episode.

Folk wisdom says, "Don't count your chickens before they are hatched." If and when they hatch, then we can decide who gets the tax cut.

SUBLIMINAL POLITICAL ADVERTISEMENTS

September 19, 2000

On the *McLaughlin Group* on PBS, Tony Blankley said, "Presidential campaigns are mistakes recovered from." Was *The Kiss* one of those mistakes? This is what Al Gore gave Tipper at the Democratic Convention. Paul Greenberg called it "another moment of mild depravity." Somebody else advised, "Get a room!" On the other hand, it was *family values*. Al Gore said to America, "I love my wife," evidently a message he thought needed to be sent. On the whole, let's give it a plus.

On *Hardball*, there was theorizing that in the end, the Nader vote will go to Al Gore. Guest Democratic Rep. Barney Frank continues, "Pat Buchanan's 2% remains an irreducible minimum of very mean people." I predict that this year, "mean" will not resonate with voters.

Ed Gillespie, Republican lobbyist who recently joined the Bush campaign strategists in Austin, spoke of Al Gore's proposals as "wasteful Washington spending," a well-worn phrase, hardly original with him. Oh well, why not? The phrase has certainly worked for them before.

In the annals of presidential campaigns, this may come to be known as "the Year of the Rat." In a negative ad run by the RNC, the word "rat" appeared for 1/30th of a second, a technique often used by advertising agencies to give subliminal messages not registered by the conscious mind. This message, however, was registered by plenty of conscious minds. Senate minority leader Tom Daschle called a press conference on behalf of the Democratic leaders and said, "We smell a rat." The RNC denied intentionally placing it there, and George Bush is convinced this is true. Theories to the contrary are "bizarre." This was simply a subliminal message not intentionally sent.

On *BBC*, there was a discussion of high petrol prices, fuel shortages, and alternative energy sources. One Brit opined brightly, "It's too bad all of the hot air generated in political contests can't be harnessed into energy. Then we would never have to worry about the depletion of fossil fuels."

The comedian Chris Rock, when asked if he had any observations about the current presidential contest, said, "Whoever messes up last is gonna lose." That's prophetic!

WHAT'S A FAIR TAX?

September 21, 2000

By definition, governments tax. It is part of the job description. The problem then becomes how to make taxing fair, equitable, and probably even harder, how to achieve compliance.

Russia, a fledgling democracy, is trying to tax, but people aren't used to the concept, so they hardly see the point. We have plenty of tax loopholes for the very rich, but practically all of their nouveau riche manage to pay absolutely nothing.

Our problems with the Internal Revenue Service are pretty systemic, so that people speak of overhauling it or abolishing it altogether. Many present members of Congress are beating this drum. The present chairman of the Ways and Means Committee in the House of Representatives, Republican Pete Dominici, openly says he plans to tear the IRS out by the roots so that it will never come back.

One problem is that forms and tax codes are so complicated that almost anyone who fills out the long form needs a tax accountant. The complexity of the tax forms is not the fault of the IRS, but of Congress, which every year passes amendments added to amendments added to amendments.

Ten million people do not pay taxes each year because they do not file the tax forms. It's The Great American Tax Dodge, and the number of cheaters grows larger year after year. Who are these miscreants? Many are incredibly rich people who own multiple homes in countries all over the world.

At the other end, there are 10% of folk who are self-employed, operate in a strict cash economy and pay no taxes. Every year, more and more people slip into this category because they see other folk doing it with apparent success.

Probably the biggest problem the IRS has is that Congress has not adequately funded it in several years. They refuse to appropriate money for studies on who these deadbeats are, or money to go after them.

The scandals of recent years were about the IRS going after middle-class America. Houses and cars were impounded. A premium was paid to workers who could come up with huge numbers of violators. There was more incentive to go after lots of little guys rather than a few really rich folk who could hire smart lawyers or had a friendly congressman in their pockets.

Steve Forbes, Republican candidate for president, ran on a platform of a flat tax of 15% for everyone across the board, with no exemptions. Of course, this plan would have been great for Steve Forbes. Some suggest that the solution might be a flat tax, but graduated so that the richest would still pay the most, again with no exemptions. We would have to give up all of our deductions for mortgage, age, contributions to charity . . . everything. This would be pretty hard to do, but we might be better off, and we could get it all on one page.

MEETING OF THE FEMALE MINDS ON LARRY KING LIVE

September 23, 2000

The format for a recent Larry King program was a panel of six guests, each of whom briefly answered a number of questions. The guests were women: three Republicans, three Democrats, and all well-known. The Democrats were Maya Angelou, author and poet; Sally Jesse Raphael, talk show host; and Senator Mary Landrieu of Louisiana. The Republicans were Bo Derek, Hollywood actress; Rep. Mary Bono of California; and Loretta Lynn, country singer.

Maya Angelou answered every question in beautiful poetry prose. Mary Landrieu and Sally Jesse Raphael gave answers very much as I would have given. We were in sync.

I had wondered about Mary Bono. I had not seen or heard from her since the impeachment hearings, and was glad to see she was surviving in the big leagues. Evidently, she has been elected over and over again by adoring constituents. She is very beautiful, the most beautiful of the six, and her face reminded me of Teresa Wright, well-known actress of the '40s. Bono was confident and self-assured, and gave answers which we have heard for twenty years. "I am for George Bush because he will give us smaller government, less regulation, and lower taxes." She had that down pat. Guess she didn't need anything else.

Bo Derek is surviving in great shape—maybe even still a "10." She was for George Bush for whatever well-known reasons.

Loretta Lynn spoke in a deep southern accent, as she would have to do to sing country. She was for George Bush because the morals of America are so low. If George Bush isn't elected—she left the rest for us to finish. This we know . . . it was most dire. George Bush would be the savior. He would save the country from godless Democrats!

All six women were pro-choice. At one point, Jesse Raphael said to Loretta Lynn, "Do you want a bunch of men telling you what you can do with your body?" Lynn replied, "No man is ever going to tell me what to do with my body."

Bo Derek said, "Roe v. Wade is not ever going to be overturned, ever, ever, ever. We are never going back to 'those days'." All three Republican women wanted to see the abortion plank removed from their platform.

Loretta Lynn goes way back with the Bushes. In the '80s, she rode the bus with George Bush, Sr. as he campaigned. Of his opponent, she said at the time, "I can't even pronounce his name [Dukakis]." She represents a whole block of voters in the Deep South. I wonder how they're doing with Hadassah.

OIL SHORTAGE

September 24, 2000

How does the oil shortage impact the present political contest? Will the brouhaha benefit Bush or Gore? Neither, I should hope.

If Al Gore is in favor of Clinton's move to tap into our strategic reserves in order to assure there will be enough heating oil to keep our neighbors to the north from freezing this winter, isn't it rather craven to impinge Clinton's motives?

On the other hand, George Bush was in the oil business a number of years ago and got out of it after having lost money, so how in the world is he a part of any big oil conspiracy? Dick Cheney was with Halliburton until recently, and you might make a case for conflict of interest, but conspiracy? No.

I live in an oil town, and I have seen Phillips Petroleum Company operate in good times and bad, through Wall Street raiders T. Boone Pickens and Carl Icahn. I've known the people who worked there, and I have pretty close connections myself. I do not think they have ever tried to do anything except operate a profitable business, which is what all companies do.

If oil prices had not stayed in the tank for so long, we would not have abandoned all our domestic production and would not be so dependent on foreign oil.

My siblings and I own mineral rights to some property in Washita County. A geologist member of the family assures us there is no oil to be found in the part of the county where our property is located, although considerable amounts have been found in other parts of the county. I still theorize that if things get bad enough, techniques will be developed to drill deeper and find oil in my part of that county. If this happened, it would in no way be the culmination of a conspiracy on my part.

These same siblings and I own mineral rights to property in Kay County where there has been enough gas production in other years that it showed up as a blip on our income taxes. The last check I received was for ninety cents a number of years ago. A brother and a sister had already transferred ownership of their shares to their children. I have often laughed, thinking of the checks those nieces and nephews received that year. What are the chances of getting rich on oil as opposed to striking it rich on the lottery? Keep buying those lottery tickets. On the other hand, keep reactivating those rigs.

THE WORLD'S POWER MONGERS

September 25, 2000

I am so proud of the Serbian people! What a thing to have said at any time in the last 12 years! Since the death of Tito, Slobodan Milosevich has, with the help of the army and the police, kept the populace abjectly under heel. He is responsible for thousands of deaths in Bosnia, Croatia and Kosovo. He was the one who invented ethnic cleansing as a way to unify the Serbs, and gain and hold power.

Except for the intervention of our brave men, and those of other nations, he would have continued to sow hatred and division, and to maim and slaughter all across Europe. Sanctions have worked, and because of them, the actions of NATO, the UN, and everyone in the free world, a climate has been created in which the Serbian people could show this courage and live to tell the tale. They have voted out of power the invincible Milosevich.

I'm glad for the Peruvians too. Alberto Fujimori, after his election in 1990, accomplished many good things for this battered, bruised and beleaguered country. He stopped triple-digit inflation, stopped the wholesale abduction of children, and instituted some semblance of democracy.

But, he came authoritarian and corrupt. His chief deputy, Montecinos, was shown in a video offering a bribe to a congressman. Beware the technological age. Technology protects us all. To the credit of the Peruvian people, they expressed their outrage and demanded accounting. Fujimori has announced he will step down, and Montecinos has left the country in disgrace. This is progress. In the history of Peru, many bloody events have gone unchronicled and unavenged.

In Indonesia, at long last, the people are holding the Suharto family accountable for the treasure they have plundered from the country over many years.

We have often wondered why the Iraqi people allow Saddam Hussein to remain in brutal power, unchallenged. Remember, he rose to power because he was the bloody hatchetman to several of his predecessors. In Iraq, you can't be a hero. Long before you reach that status, you'll be dead.

VIOLENCE IN ENTERTAINMENT

September 26, 2000

Free speech, artistic expression, pornography, corruption, redemption. How is a free society to reconcile all of these irreconcilable concepts into something positive?

Does watching violence breed violence? Should we permit the entertainment industry to produce a product demoralizing to our society, particularly to our youth, and even to our children? Do entertainment products indeed do this? Is it the parents' fault if they fail to protect their children? Is it humanly possible for them to protect their children in such an environment?

It is my opinion that the entertainment industry does produce products which contribute to the delinquency of our youth. Maybe "adult" entertainment isn't corrupting to adults, but exposing children to it might be criminal.

A recent newspaper story about the profane white rapper Eminem and his mentor addressed this very point. The mentor said, "It's just music. It's artistic expression. That's all it's supposed to be." In other words, what's the big deal?

Of course, watching violence breeds violence. Of course, parents should protect their children from inappropriate material. But, in a society saturated with the seductive and salacious, these parents face an impossible task, and even with the utmost vigilance, many will fail. Why am I so positive? Because I have experienced it firsthand. I have seen it happen.

What I am not so positive about is what we can do about it. But please, society, let's grapple! Let's grapple!

A KINDER, GENTLER NEWT

September 29, 2000

Guess what? Newt Gingrich is mellowing. I caught a panel discussion on *C-Span*, on which very erudite public figures were discussing the "Clinton Years." Included in the participants were Senator Paul Wellstone (D-Minn.), Newt Gingrich, former Republican Speaker of the House (and in many ways President Clinton's nemesis), and several journalists. Norm Ornstein was moderator, and it was indeed a lively evening.

What I distilled from the exchange was that Newt Gingrich was actually likable, non-confrontational and objective in his remarks. Having fallen from grace, he no longer has to strategize, spin or evangelize. He gave Clinton his due, much more so than Paul Wellstone, who thought however well things were done, they could have been done better.

Gingrich has also been known, of late, to defend Al Gore. He said that while a senator, Gore was about the only senator who knew anything about the technology of creating the Internet. He certainly was the most knowledgeable.

That's coming a long way from the Gingrich who, in the early '90s, boasted that he intended to let Medicare "wither on the vine." He was going to restore American civilization by bombing big government into oblivion.

Americans seem to like divided government. It's a government of checks and balances. Some of the "big spending" was done when we had Democrats in the White House and in control of Congress. Those times gave us Social Security, Medicare, unemployment insurance, etc. Someone had said if, God forbid, we had a Republican president and a Republican-controlled congress, they would roll back the 20th century.

Gingrich strutted and fretted his way across the stage for some pretty interesting years, but you can't say he will be heard from no more. He's still around, sadder perhaps, but also mellower . . . and certainly $4.5 million poorer.

PAT ROBERTSON AND THE VOTER GUIDES

September 30, 2000

The Christian Coalition is now in convention in Washington D.C., and George Bush elected not to address the body. Pat Robertson is visibly annoyed, so behind the scenes, he's probably furious.

George Bush did decide to send a surrogate, Lynn Cheney, wife of the Republican vice presidential candidate, Dick Cheney. She has already, as you can imagine, very effectively addressed the body. The message sent in every possible way by Pat Robertson to George Bush was "Don't take us for granted."

Ultimately, Candidate Bush did address the coalition by satellite on Saturday.

Robertson says that 70 million voter guides are ready to mail, and I am sure the organization still maintains a tax-exempt status (as a religious rather than political organization).

Polls and focus groups find that women, rather than saying, "Get government off my back," are saying, "Get government *on my side*." Year 2000 census figures show that there are fewer people in poverty now than in the last 21 years. Somebody must be doing something right.

As far as "getting the hand of government out of your pockets" goes, so that *you* can spend *your* money like *you* want to, can you imagine Mr. Individual Taxpayer deciding to spend his money filling a pothole or shoring up a crumbling schoolhouse?

To those who worry that, despite Pat Robertson, his legions and voter guides, George Bush might be running no better than neck-and-neck, or even sometimes behind, Mark Shields says, "Cheer up. The economy might get worse."

ARIEL SHARON AND THE PEACE PROCESS

October 1, 2000

What Ariel Sharon has just done is the outrage of the century. He has taken the fragile peace negotiations between the Israelis and the Palestinians, which have taken years to evolve to this point, and set them back light years.

Among the most emotionally charged points of difference in the negotiations are the holy places in Jerusalem and who should have jurisdiction over them. Sharon, together with about one hundred hardlined right-wingers, stormed the temple mount, one of those disputed places. This action was done for one reason and one reason only: to provoke the Palestinians and wreak havoc. The resulting mayhem did not disappoint.

The Palestinians were provoked, several rock-throwing incidents have been met with gunfire, and the list of Palestinian casualties grows and grows.

Politically, Ariel Sharon's party is out of power, he disapproves of what Barak and his predecessor have accomplished toward peace, and Sharon has set about to sabotage the whole process.

What is the solution to this most insoluble problem? When this was being discussed years ago, my good friend Elizabeth Hughes said she believed that the whole process of displacing the

Palestinians in order to give the Israelis a homeland was a mistake. This is where I stand now.

But having done this, where do we go from here? I am so glad the Christians are not fighting the same battle over Jerusalem. After all, it is our Holy City, too.

In a discussion about this the other day, Phil Lorenz said, tongue-in-cheek (or so I thought), "A solution might be just to bomb Jerusalem. After all, we do not worship a place; we worship a Person." If there is no longer a place, the question of jurisdiction over that place would be moot.

Right now, this solution seems too extreme to take seriously. I wonder if, fifty years from now, it will seem, while not a reasonable thing to do, the last option.

WHOM DO YOU DISLIKE THE LEAST?

October 18, 2000

As a voter, I was decided long before the candidates were winnowed out. With me, it was never a matter of whom was folksier, who seemed most at home in my living room, or who had the winningest smile. For this reason, I feel much greater kinship with those "decideds" of the other persuasion than I do with the "swings."

I can't imagine anyone living and breathing in America throughout the years, or even year, not having an ideological leaning one way or the other. How can it be that someone does not know whether or not he favors an activist government, a woman's right to choose, whether he is for the poor or the rich, or whether he considers taxes necessary or Machiavellian?

Apart from ideology, I can't imagine anyone not being familiar with the two candidates by now. What is it he doesn't know about Al Gore and George W.?

For the primaries, the candidates went to the extreme left or right to shore up their bases. Then they both came to the center to appeal to the undecideds. These must include people who have never voted and have no political memory bank whatsoever. Sometimes I suspect the campaign spiels are even targeting a few aliens from outer space. Eighty percent of campaign rhetoric aimed at those undecideds is pure drivel, as in the news coverage that follows. Much of it is an insult to the intelligence of those of us who actually lived the '50s, '60s, '70s, etc., and know what happened and how the present came to be. We already know what we believe and how we will vote, but very little meat is thrown our way.

I keep my channel changer handy, and when some network assembles a focus group of undecideds, euphemistically referred to as "real people," I switch in a hurry to anything else—anything except people offering opinions based upon absolute trivia.

A panel on *Larry King Live* was discussing the vice presidential debates, and someone said, "Cheney was so good, he made George Bush look bad." John Kasich said, "Leiberman looked so good, he made Al Gore look bad." Mario Cuomo said, "The question is, who made who look worse?"

After the second presidential candidates' debate, a panel of historians was discussing the score. It was agreed that both participants accomplished what they needed to accomplish. Richard Norton Smith summed it up for all of them when he said, "Gore came across as less annoying, and Bush was more coherent."

Whether it's Cheney Mania, Bush Malapropisms, Lieberman's Holier-Than-Thou, or Gore's School Teacherisms, there is something for everyone to dislike. If nothing else, you undecideds, decide whom you dislike the least.

THE PUBLIC
RELATIONS WAR

November 21, 2000

On a recent British Broadcasting panel discussion, a journalist from Ireland proposed, tongue in cheek, that the whole world should be permitted to vote for the President of the United States, because that person would, in fact, be president of the whole world.

A similar story came out of Russia. It seems that in a local election in some Russian town, people were permitted to cast votes for our presidential candidates. A young man was shown very seriously telling why he voted for George Bush. "He says he would do something about criminals in our country stealing from our government."

For the past week, all eyes have been on Florida, and in my opinion, the Sunshine State comes off looking pretty good: the openness of all procedures, the wonderful people counting votes around the clock, and the diligence of the Florida Supreme Court.

After election night, hundreds of lawyers descended upon Florida, and a few really did argue in some Florida courts. Ted Olson (of impeachment fame) spoke for the Republican Party, but only once that I heard, and then he was correctly put into a lockbox. He came off looking like Attila the Hun, and his wife Barbara (a talk show celebrity) like Mrs. Attila the Hun. Public relations-wise, Olson was a disaster, but so was James Baker, still speaking furiously and vitriolically for the Republican Party.

Who wins the public relations war is important. At first it was George Bush, convinced by Dan Rather that he had been elected. Everyone was saying Al Gore was a sore loser, and at some point, for the good of the country, why didn't he just concede? Now it looks like Gore has a fighting chance, and at some point, for the good of the country, shouldn't George Bush just concede?

But the guy who ran a whole campaign on his trust of the people and the superior wisdom of the states in all things doesn't trust the people to count votes or the state of Florida to call an election.

The Republicans have a new star—Marc Racicot, Governor of Montana. His is a new face, a pleasant face, and his spin is great. Katharine Harris, Florida Secretary of State, has earned her spurs for the Republican Party, and will undoubtedly have full party support in her bid for the Senate.

Now we all know about the whole universe of chads, hanging "pregnant, dimpled and pimpled," the latter a coinage of Bob Dole, and which has now been fully accepted into our lexicography.

NO ONE WON THIS ELECTION

December 5, 2000

They won. We lost. We appeal. Those were the words of David Bois, chief counsel for Gore forces, as Circuit Judge N. Sanders Sauls handed down the verdict which ruled negative for them on every plea.

Today, the scales definitely tip toward a Bush presidency, and here are some sobering consequences of such an eventuality. Republican Senator Strom Thurmond is now 98 years old and is the third heartbeat away from the presidency. He is in line after Dick Cheney, would-be vice president, who is two weeks away from his fourth heart attack. *NPR* is currently running a series on wonderfully articulate centenarians, but Strom Thurmond would not qualify as one. His southern accent is so thick, even if he said something terribly erudite, I wouldn't know. "Hewehalushshet" ("Have we had lunch yet?") My impression is that his aides have to propel him through the halls of Congress, one on each side. On the other hand, at the age of 98, he does well to even show up for work.

The format for most talk shows is to have two protagonists on each side of every issue. On *Geraldo Rivera* these days, the same lawyers who tell us in legalese just why Bush won the election are the same ones who used to tell us why Bill Clinton should be impeached. It is chilling to hear them tell how it would be perfectly legal for the Florida legislature to decide whom our next president will be by appointing their own slate of 25 electors.

The same is true of members of Congress. They are the same old impeachment faces: Trent Lott, Orrin Hatch, Dick Armey and Tom Delay. If what will be needed first is reaching across the aisle and extending olive branches, I suggest to the recipients of such overtures to extend their hands but watch their backs.

Let's face it. No one won this election. It was a tie. Cokie Roberts in her column suggests this mantra be embroidered in needlepoint and hung in the Oval Office. It was a toss of the coin, and Judge N. Sanders Sauls called it, for now.

COUNT THE VOTES
FOR HISTORY

December 13, 2000

I would like to write counterpoint to the assumptions of the Republican party. By them, it was generally assumed that if Al Gore won this election, there would be blood in the streets, but if George Bush won, Democrats would be so mesmerized by his charisma, they would all immediately start purring like kittens.

Robert Reich, former Secretary of Labor, said he found the sentiments among Democrats to run the gamut from outrage to outrage.

I heard Bob Michel, Republican minority leader of the House in pre-Gingrich days, speaking of his anticipation of the Bush ascendancy. Soft-spoken and glowing beatifically, he spoke of this remarkable young man who could just work with Democrats and bring everybody together.

Jennifer Dunn, House-R, said it this way. First, she showed two fists and then an entwining of the fingers. This is the magic the Bush alchemy will bring about. Other hard-bitten Republican operatives have expressed the same thing less convincingly.

In accomplishing this assignment, the difficult part for Bush will be handling his "bad boys" in Congress. Tom Delay has talked early and loud about the Republican clean sweep of the Congress and White House. Now they can really get something done! Some of these guys are constitutionally unentwinable. George Bush, for the good of the country, muzzle this guy if you can.

The second assumption is that the votes have been counted, and counted and counted. This is the spin the Republicans all repeated and repeated and repeated. No Democrat ever bought it. It's like trying to resolve something over the telephone and never being allowed to talk to a real live person.

I heard a caller to *C-Span* saying, "If they are allowed to count those votes, Gore will win, and that just isn't fair!" Duh! But Antonin Scalia said the same thing. A recount would do irreparable harm to George Bush. Of course. As the four dissenting members of the Court pointed out, not to manually recount the votes will do irreparable harm to Al Gore.

One thing we know for sure, the members of the Supreme Court don't like each other very much. Someone has predicted that with a Senate so evenly divided, any vacancies on the Supreme Court might well last for years.

A suggestion has been made to count the votes now, not for the purpose of determining this election, but for history. That's where I weigh in.

THE CARDS WERE STACKED

December 16, 2000

That George Bush is a committed Christian is certainly obvious to all, and I like that he asked for American's prayers for his administration, and that all families get involved in this political contest. The statement he made that everything happens for a purpose is something I am chewing over, because, in general, those are not the terms that I apply to events. It is a little like predestination, which has truth in the big picture, but on the other hand, there is free will.

There is also the luck of the draw. This contest had to come down to Florida, with a Republican legislature, but only of very recent date; and Katharine Harris, in the position of Secretary of State, a job scheduled to be abolished by the year 2002. She was co-chair for George Bush's Florida campaign and had several discretionary calls which she assiduously called for Bush. There was brother Jeb Bush, who, as governor, was scheduled to sign several crucial documents, and of course, he was pledged to deliver Florida.

There were Florida's antiquated voting machines, confusing ballots, and the time constraints. Florida, this is the second time you have goofed up elections. Three generations hence, don't make us go through this again!

Ah, the time constraints. These allowed the strategy of running out the clock, the absolute slam-dunk maneuver of the whole campaign. The maneuver probably would have worked anyway, but it was tailor-made for the U.S. Supreme Court to come in the last two seconds of the game and throw that ball into the hoop. They wore the Republican colors, and now we know for sure whose team they were on. No politics involved in their deliberations, Clarence Thomas? No way they can convince America they were only the umpires.

If all of those actualities converged because of some great cosmic plan, we won't be able to divine it for at least a thousand years, and then some 31st-century James Burke will have to show us the connections.

Poor Al Gore. He couldn't win for losing. Poor us 50%. The cards were stacked.

ONE MAN, ONE VOTE

December 17, 2000

I would like to address the anachronism of the electoral college. It was first intended by our founding fathers that only the elite govern, so they went to elaborate means to insure that the proletariat participated in no way in the governing, even to the extent of voting on which of the elite got to govern.

At first, owning property was a requisite of voting. If you owned a mule, you could vote. If the mule died before the next election, you couldn't vote. It was not until early in the 20th century that women were granted voting privileges. The Voting Rights Act was passed only mid-century, during the presidency of Lyndon Johnson. Even in America, universal suffrage is still pretty new, but "one man, one vote" is now the way we do it, and the way we think it should be done.

Except in Florida. There, in practice, they revert back to theory that the elite should govern; therefore, regardless of what the voters say, the legislature must be the final arbiter. Having decided what the final outcome should be, they will find whatever law they need, even if they have to go back to caveman days. At some point, if laws don't make sense, should they be *law*?

The founding fathers were pretty smart, and they gave us a Constitution like the Rock of Gibraltar. We have a Supreme Court to keep us in line with the intentions of the writers of that document. But isn't it conceivable that we might, sometime and about something, move beyond them? In this instance, shouldn't "one man, one vote" prevail?

I am sure all of these smart lawyers talking about the Constitution cringe to think that women, blacks, Haitians, Mexicans, or immigrants who can't speak English each have a vote equal to any one of them. But that's the way it is, and maybe that fact is what in the end will let the glory out.

WISH HE WERE
A DEMOCRAT

December 27, 2000

Colin Powell, as Secretary of State, will be one of the most powerful men in the world. I will be glad to see him wield that power.

He captivated the minds and hearts of the American people as Chief of Staff during the Gulf War. We had the feeling that he was the sort of person to whom we would want to entrust the winning of the war.

In his military days, he never tipped his hand as to his political affiliations, and indeed, it is my impression he made that choice after he left the military. Either party would have been glad to have him as their standard-bearer in a presidential contest, and he could have been Secretary of State under a Gore administration as well.

I will never understand why he chose to be a Republican. In his younger days, he suffered all the indignities all blacks suffered in a racist society. He loved the military because it was the one place he was allowed to shine. The Republican Party has never done anything for blacks. The Democratic Party pushed civil rights, voting rights, and affirmative action. Right now, in Florida, Jeb Bush has just finished abolishing affirmative action, piece by piece.

Colin Powell is pro-choice, and although the Jerry Falwells would never criticize him as they have Christy Todd Whitman, they are glad that his cabinet post is not Education, or Health and Human Services.

Powell couldn't prostitute himself as you have to do to raise money to run for office, and he could never appease the Religious Right or the Republican revolutionaries still around from the Gingrich years.

Powell didn't show up in Crawford wearing Gucci Western, as did Trent Lott and others. "I don't do ranchwear very well," he said. And here this tough general who could win a war, said, "I grew up in the South Bronx. I don't care what you say, those cows look dangerous."

He doesn't have the temperament for bloody political brawls, and who does? But he's a take-charge kind of guy, and having been appointed to a position of power, he's going to stride in and take on the world.

SOMETHING'S GOTTA GIVE

December 30, 2000

President Clinton, in his latest proposals to the Israelis and Palestinians, spoke the unspeakable, touched the untouchable, and dared the impossible. Jurisdiction over Jerusalem and resolution of the Palestinian refugee problem have been matters so highly charged and fraught with explosive emotion that they have been continually shoved back, not talked about, and left until later. Now it *is* later, and Clinton has put them both on the table, talked about them out loud, and made proposals.

Israel would give up jurisdiction of the Temple Mount, Muslim's most holy place, and Palestinians would give up expectation of returning to Israel. Of course, each knows they cannot get everything they want, and that if there is ever a peace agreement, each must give up something. Deal with the intractable, the irresistible force, the immovable object. Something's gotta give, something's gotta give, something's gotta give.

Today, there are four million Palestinians living in refugee camps who are descendants of those dispossessed 50 years ago in order to form the state of Israel. Although I believe this dispossession was absolutely a mistake to begin with, it is completely unrealistic to think that today, the Palestinians could return, four million strong, to live in Israel.

Under Clinton's proposals, there would be a Palestinian state, with Israel ceding to the Palestinians all of the Gaza Strip and 95% of the West Bank. Israel would keep 5% for its settlements. Palestinians should certainly be uncontested in their right to live in Gaza and the West Bank, and Israel should stop policing them, enacting curfews and restricting movement. It is unfortunate that the Palestinians are so dependent upon the Israelis economically, but surely, in time that will change for the better.

No one in the world knows more about this millennial problem than Bill Clinton, and I have the feeling that this solution is as good at it's gonna get. Yasser Arafat pretends not to understand completely. Bill Clinton says everybody knows exactly what is set forth in the proposals. At last, we're down to bedrock. The unspeakable has now been spoken. It's up to everyone to give a little.

OKLAHOMA PRIDE

January 5, 2001

Somewhere moldering in a lockbox lies a scrap of paper from long ago: a baccalaureate degree from OU. It gives me license to glow with pride every time our football team wins a national championship. Otherwise, sports are not my package. The Orange Bowl game even had smiling Governor Frank Keating giving Oklahoma a "thumbs up."

This win was special in many ways. Head coach Bob Stoops accomplished the victory in only his second year at OU. He is truly a person to write about.

I like to listen to a panel on *NPR* every week called *Business World*, a group of professors from TU discussing all of the new, new things. Their assessment of the game was most interesting. They quoted Bob Stoops as saying "My father would be more proud of me because of the way I treat my family and friends than of my success as a coach."

This panel of clever, funny guys gave credit for Stoops' success as a coach to the fact that he is a nice guy: nice to his coaches, nice to his players, nice to everyone. Now that is a switch! Remember, only last year, legendary basketball coach Bobby Knight of the University of Indiana made news for exactly the opposite reason. His authority as a coach was established by way of a fiery temper and frequent outbursts which left his players cowering. After repeated warnings that the tirades were unacceptable, the university reluctantly fired their winningest coach.

Meanwhile, back in Stoops' Country, one of the OU coaches had a wife in the hospital due to give birth to triplets. Stoops arranged a jet to fly this coach back to Norman ahead of schedule so he'd be home in time for the births.

Knowledgeable people say that Florida State actually had the best athletes, man for man. What OU had was team play which was so spectacular, they made *the men* look like rookies.

Instead of belittling and bullying his players in order to motivate them, as coaches do all across the spectrum, from Little League to professional, Stoops accomplishes his magic by a friendly, positive approach which leaves every player feeling good about himself. According to the panel, this approach works in business too.

Not known for my collection of sports memorabilia, I hope soon to be sporting a Sooner Orange Bowl sweatshirt. To the bone, I'm a Sooner born and a Sooner bred, and when I die, I'll be a Sooner dead. Rah! Rah! Oklahoma! Rah! Rah! Oklahoma!

PAY DOWN THE DEBT

January 8, 2001

A lan Greenspan raised interest rates six times in the year 2000 in order to slow down an overheated economy. So successful was he in slowing down the economy that he was wont to stage a dramatic reversal toward the end of December by lowering interest rates by one-half of a percentage point.

George Bush and Dick Cheney campaigned on a trillion-dollar tax cut because people should decide how to spend their own money, and the people who pay the taxes (the millionaires and billionaires) should be the ones to get the money back. Maybe they'd rather play the horses and let someone else fill the potholes. That should be their decision.

Now that GB and DC have been declared winners-elect, you don't hear that particular spin anymore. Now we need a tax cut to revive the economy that has just been overheating. All the time, Alan Greenspan is saying "Pay down the debt first; then cut taxes."

If the economy does go into the tank, there goes the surplus that was supposed to pay for the tax cut, and a cut would mean deficits accumulating again, rather than surpluses. George the First called it "voodoo economics" way back in the '70s, and history proved him right.

Retiring Senator Patrick Moynihan, on the talk show *Evans and Novak*, showed gentility and civility in complimenting George

Bush as a person, and praising his choice of cabinet members (even conservative John Ashcroft). Moynihan said paying down the debt would have the same beneficial effect as a tax cut and would result in a much healthier economy.

All the while, consumers are getting mixed messages. Everyone is carrying too much credit card debt, yet consumer spending is what will keep the good times rolling. If Christmas sales this year don't exceed last year's Christmas sales, the economy goes south.

Saving is a virtue and produces capital. On the other hand, spending is good for business. I say, everybody save if you can, buy what you can afford, and the free market will adjust.

POSTMORTEMS

January 13, 2001

One thing for sure, if you're speaking to a national audience about something as serious as politics, better not show any levity, because what you say will be taken seriously and literally.

I don't consider my antennae particularly sensitive, but when Al Gore, speaking to a Labor conclave, said his mother sang to him a lullaby when he was a baby, "Look for the Union Label," I knew he was kidding for the benefit of that particular audience. When Bill Clinton visited with the Daley brothers in Chicago and said to Bill Daley, "You did a great job in helping Al Gore win the election," I considered it camaraderie, and did not think he was challenging George Bush's legitimacy as president.

Republicans, your man will be inaugurated. Please allow us losers our postmortems.

Now I will change the subject to political spin and double-talk. Jack Germond, a 40-year reporter for the *Baltimore Sun* (25 of those years as a political reporter), recently announced his retirement from the political beat. He said he no longer had the stomach for said spin and double-talk. He cited the contest between George Bush and John McCain, the latter running on campaign reform. George Bush, who had never reformed anything in his life, emerged from that contest, announcing that he was a reformer with results. Later, pollsters asked which of the two candidates was a reformer, and people overwhelmingly chose George Bush.

John Ashcroft spoke at Bob Jones University and was awarded an honorary degree. What he said in that speech is being carefully dissected pursuant to his confirmation hearings for Attorney General. I heard that speech, and it is the kind of speech I hear every Sunday from my mainstream church pulpit. Ashcroft's thesis was "We have no King but Jesus." It is what you expect to hear in a sermon and was entirely appropriate for that audience. After all, there is a theological view of the world which you may hold, as Joe Lieberman does, quite apart from your secular profession, and it doesn't at all mean you are blurring the lines between church and state. Incidentally, my mainstream church is evangelical, but we don't distribute voter guides or claim to have a corner on truth.

John Ashcroft is not my kind of guy, and I am only defending what he said. Whether he was wise to appear at right-wing Bob Jones University is another question.

Levity, spin, double-talk—it's all a part of politics. It's up to each one of us to navigate the minefields.

THE ASHCROFT TEST

January 23, 2001

John Ashcroft has spent his entire political life establishing his credentials as conservative, and has been so successful in doing so that he is now considered to be to the right of Jesse Helms. There are two things that you find in the middle of the road, according to Ashcroft, "a moderate and a dead skunk. I don't want to be either one of them."

Those conservative credentials have heretofore served him well, getting him elected as a two-term governor of Missouri, state Attorney General, and U.S. Senator.

Now the position in question is the Attorney General of the United States, and being confirmed in an equally divided Senate with those right-wing credentials is extremely problematic.

When Bill Clinton presented his nominees to the Senate for confirmation in the early '90's, Ashcroft opposed them to a person, because their views were not his right-wing views. Some nominees went down because of him, and some were left dangling in the wind until he made up his mind to confirm after two years. This has come to be known as "The Ashcroft Test," and it superseded the presumption that the president was entitled to appointees who shared his views. If Ashcroft had to pass The Ashcroft Test, his nomination would now be dead.

The son of a Pentecostal preacher, Ashcroft, loyal to his roots and honorable in many ways, was nevertheless ruthless in his political dealings. He singlehandedly torpedoed the nomination of Ronnie White to the federal bench for purely political reasons. At the time, Ashcroft was in a contest with Mel Carnahan, popular governor of Missouri, for reelection to his (Ashcroft's) Senate seat. He was not above shredding White in order to make points with his conservative base.

Ashcroft deserves to be held to The Ashcroft Test. But he won't be, because that would mean George Bush would be subject to the same campaign of terror the Republicans subjected Bill Clinton to for eight years. If that happened, society would disintegrate. Now we can't have that, can we?

THE VISION THING

January 24, 2001

I watched the Bush inauguration festivities with interest and pleasure. I loved watching Ricky Martin with his white teeth and Latin moves. Count me a fan.

I love First Lady Laura Bush, the beautiful and brainy librarian, of whom it has been said there is not a partisan bone in her body. And the darling daughters! Even Republicans conceded that the Clintons had done a good job in raising Chelsea. From what we can see, George and Laura have done a great job raising twins Jenna and Barbara. We shall all take pleasure in the occasional glimpses we have of them as time unfolds.

George Bush almost preached a sermon in his inaugural address. "If we see a wounded man lying by the side of the road, we will not pass by on the other side." That from a Republican! I could not believe it! Maybe this Bush has the vision thing that evaded his father. Or maybe all of this talk means a kinder, gentler nation with its hundred points of light, generated by volunteerism and the good church people of America.

I have heard it said that part of the rationale of the *big* tax cut is, as it was with Ronald Reagan, to shrink the size of the government so that there will be nothing left to spend on people progress (corporate welfare, star wars, military, and pork, of course—just not people).

The first order of business for George Bush was to return to the Reagan doctrine of not funding with tax money any family planning overseas. This means that millions of women in China and all over the world will have no information about contraception or access to women's health services of any kind. And for this information and these services, they are clamoring desperately! Does it make sense, with the population explosion and the overcrowding of the planet, that we say to people, "propagate, propagate"? The decision to cancel this program, which was reinstated early in the Clinton administration, was a bone thrown to the Religious Right and a shot across the bow warning of battles to come over Roe v. Wade.

Clinton said compassionate conservatism must include a few deeds along with the words. We shall see what vision translates to. I'm certainly not knocking this vision. You've got to have a dream. If you don't have a dream, how you gonna make your dream come true?

And now, I dispatch these letters to America with love. You can "read 'em and weep," shed nostalgic tears, applaud, rage, or shake your fist. It's democracy in dialogue. A funny thing happened as these events unfolded with this cast of characters—history happened, and we were there.

What a trip!